Norwich Ontario in Colour Photos, Saving Our History One Photo at a Time

Photography
by Barbara Raué
©2019

Series Name: Cruising Ontario

Book 243: Norwich

Cover photo: 8 Main Street East, Page 20

©All the photos in this book have been taken with my cameras. I own the rights to them.

Series Name: Cruising Ontario, Saving Our History One Photo at a Time in colour photos

Books Available in Alphabetical Order:
Aberfoyle, Acton, Ajax, Alton, Amherstburg, Ancaster, Arthur, Auburn, Aylmer, Ayr, Beaver Valley, Belfountain, Belgrave, Belleville, Bloomingdale, Blyth, Brantford, Brockville, Burford, Burgessville, Burlington, Caledon, Caledonia, Cambridge, Carlow, Cayuga, Chatsworth, Cheltenham, Clifford, Colborne, Collingwood, Conestogo, Delhi, Dorchester to Aylmer, Drayton, Drumbo, Dundas, Dunlop, Dunnville, Eden Mills, Elmira, Elora, Embro, Erin, Essex, Fergus, Fort Erie, Georgetown, Goderich, Grimsby, Guelph, Hagersville, Haldimand County, Hamilton, Hanover, Harriston, Hespeler, Ingersoll, Inglewood, Innerkip, Jarvis, Kingston, Kingsville, Kitchener, Lake Superior, Lincoln, Linwood, Listowel, London, Lucknow, Merrickville, Mono, Mount Brydges, Mount Forest, Mount Pleasant, Neustadt, New Hamburg, Newboro, Newport, Niagara-on-the-Lake, Niagara Falls, North Bay, Norwich, Oakville, Onondaga, Orangeville, Orillia, Oshawa, Otterville, Owen Sound, Palmerston, Paris, Parry Sound, Pelham, Perth, Peterborough, Petrolia, Pickering, Port Colborne, Port Elgin, Port Hope, Port Perry, Portland, Preston, Rockwood, Sarnia, Sault Ste. Marie, Seaforth, Sheffield, Shelburne, Simcoe, Smiths Falls, Smithville, Southampton, Southwest Oxford, St. Catharines, St. George, St. Jacobs, St. Marys, St. Thomas, Stoney Creek, Stouffville, Stratford, Strathroy, Sudbury, Tavistock, Terra Cotta, Thamesford, Thunder Bay, Tillsonburg, Toronto, Uxbridge, Waterdown, Waterford, Waterloo, Welland, Wellesley, West Flamborough, Westport, Whitby, Windsor, Wingham, Woodstock, York, Zorra

Book 238-239: Ingersoll
Book 240: Zorra Township
Book 241: Southwest Oxford
Book 242: Otterville, Burgessville
Book 243: Norwich
Book 244: Woodstock Book 4

Table of Contents

Stover Street	Page 4
Main Street East	Page 19
Main Street West	Page 30
Clyde Street	Page 43
John Street	Page 52
Elgin Street West	Page 58
Victoria Street	Page 61
Elgin Street East	Page 63
Cook Street	Page 64
North Court Street	Page 67
Washington Street	Page 68
Quaker Street	Page 70

In 1799, the Township of Norwich was laid out by surveyor William Hambly into lines and concessions and 200-acre lots.

In 1809, Peter Lossing, a member of the Society of Friends from Dutchess County New York, visited Norwich Township. In June 1910, with his brother-in-law Peter de Long, purchased 15,000 acres of land in this area. That fall Lossing brought his family to Upper Canada. The de Long family and nine others soon joined them. By 1820 an additional group of about fifty had settled here. These resourceful pioneers founded one of the most successful Quaker communities in Upper Canada.

The township was divided into North and South Norwich Townships in 1855.

In 1975, Oxford County underwent countywide municipal restructuring. The Village of Norwich and the Townships of East Oxford, North Norwich and South Norwich were amalgamated to create the Township of Norwich.

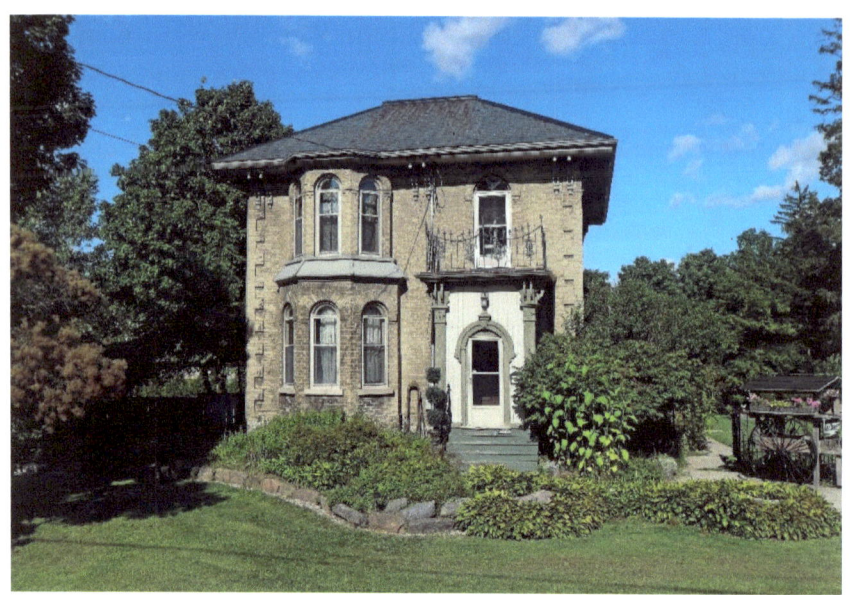

Stover Street – Italianate, hipped roof, two-story bay window, balcony above enclosed front entrance, corner quoins

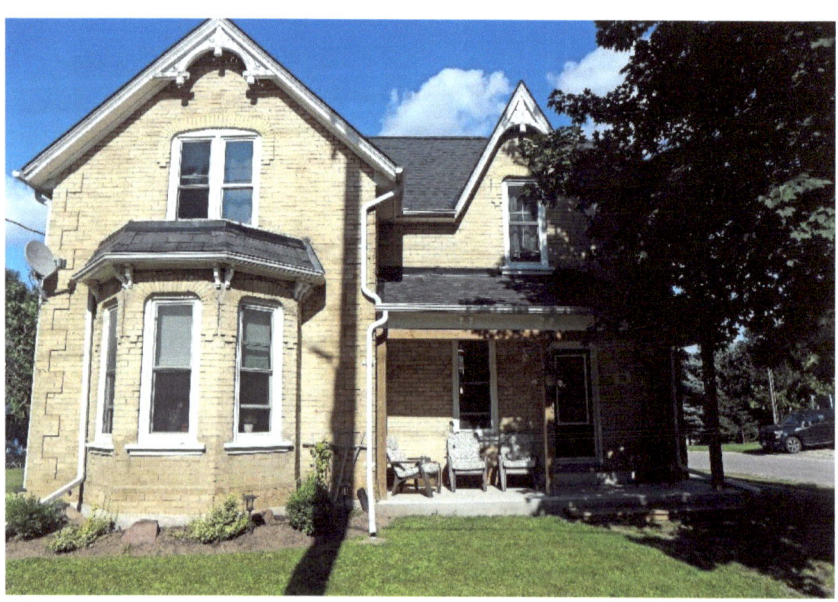

70 Stover Street – Gothic Revival, verge board trim on gables, bay window

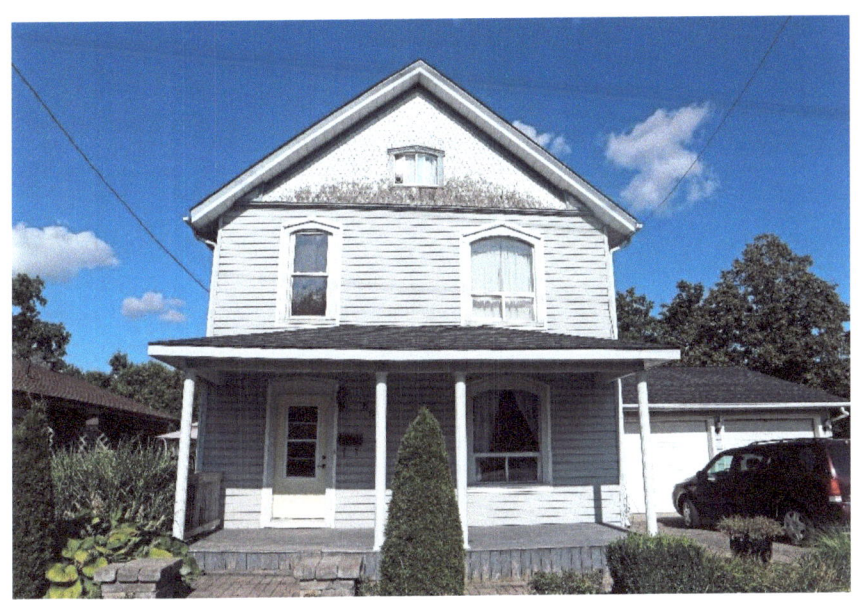

66 Stover Street

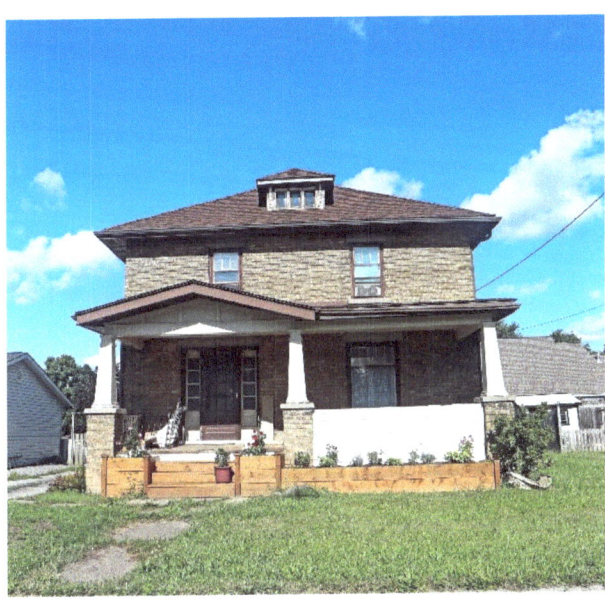

Stover Street – dormer, pediment

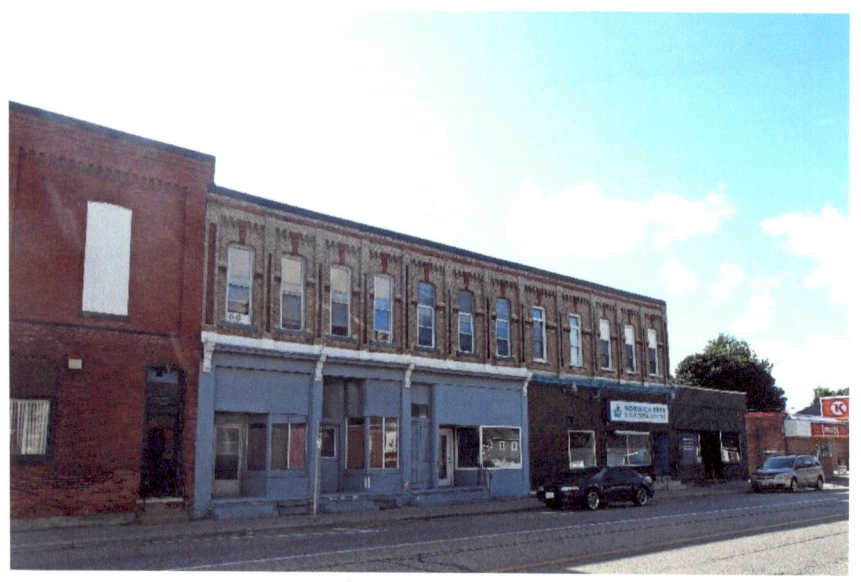

Stover Street

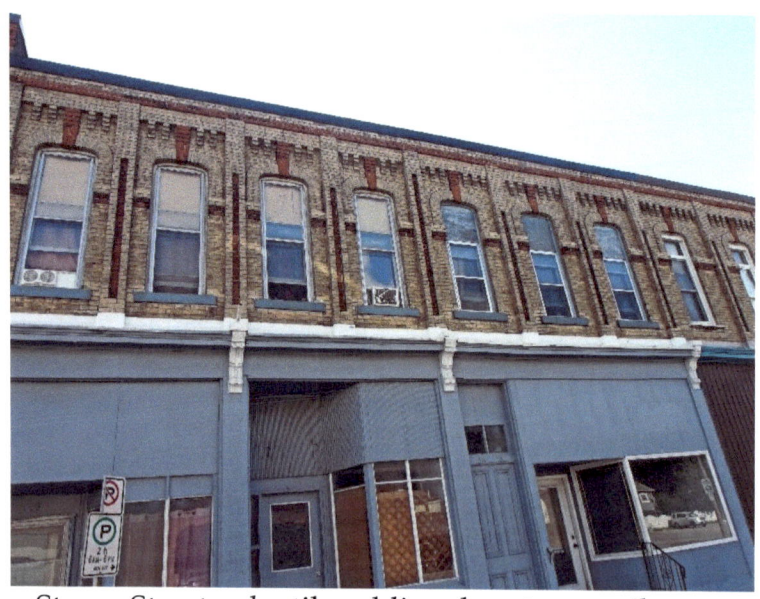

Stover Street – dentil molding, keystones, pilasters

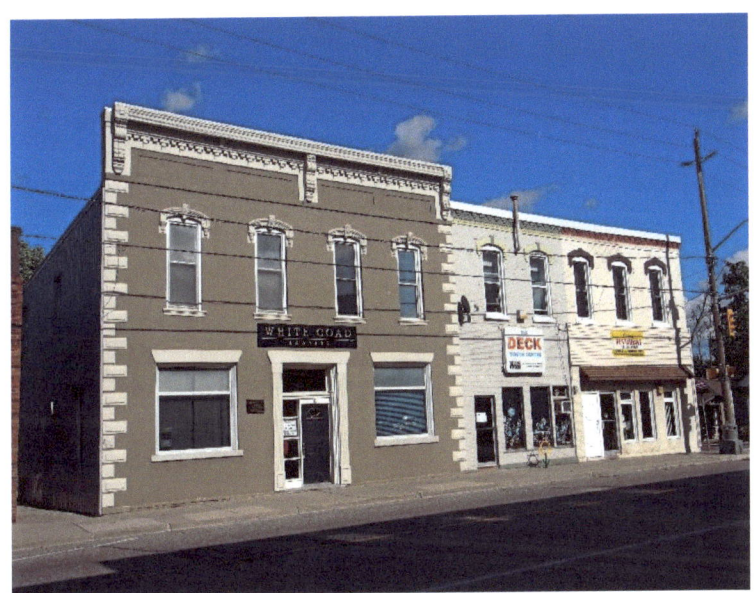

Stover Street – corner quoins, decorative cornice, keystones

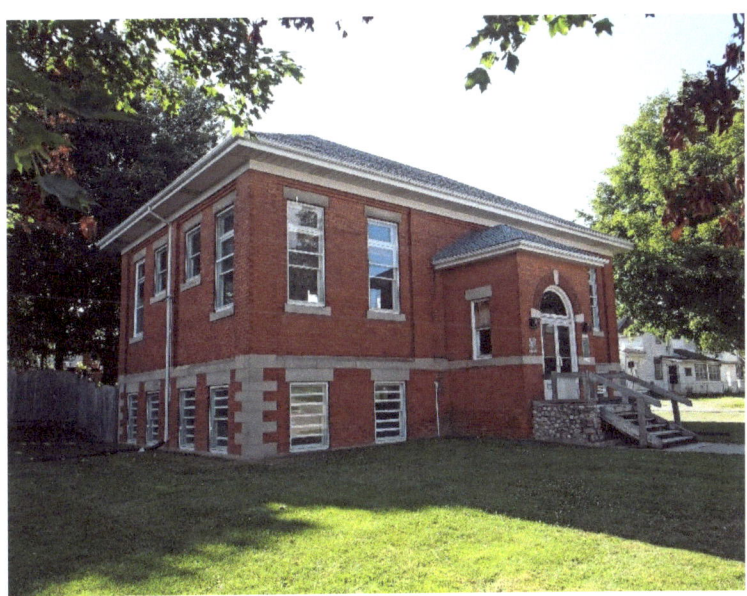

21 Stover Street North – former Oxford County Library – 1914-2006

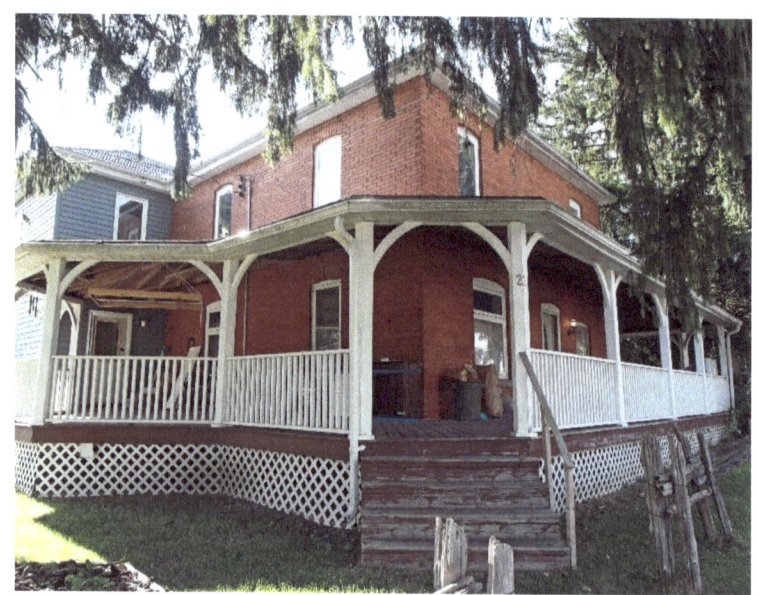
23 Stover Street – wraparound veranda

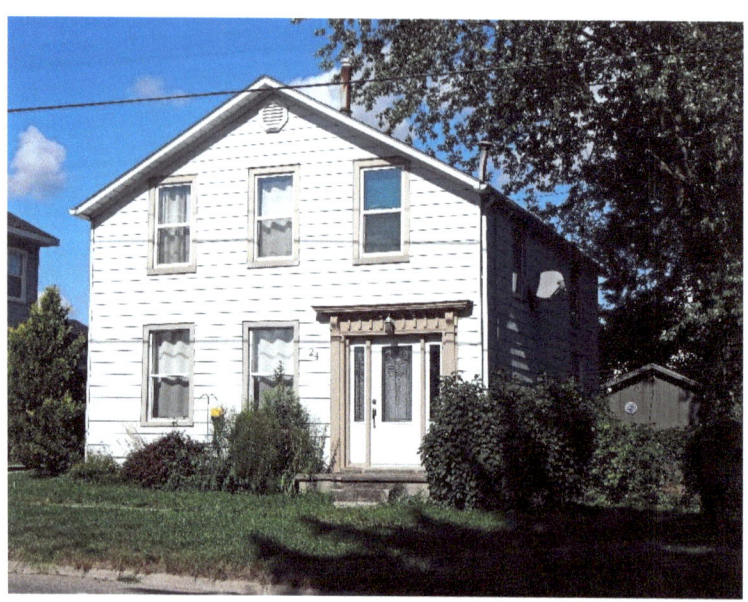
24 Stover Street - sidelights

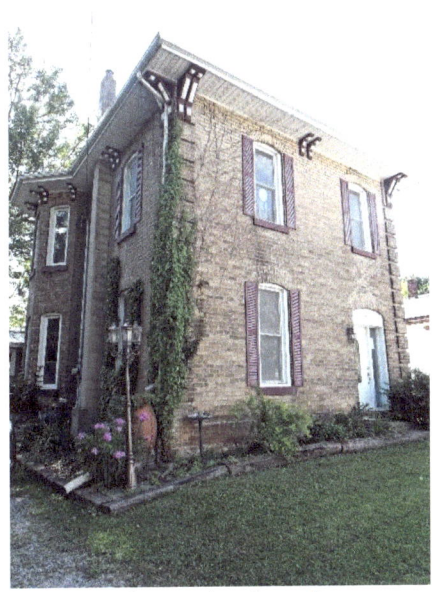

25 Stover Street – paired cornice brackets, corner quoins, bay window on side

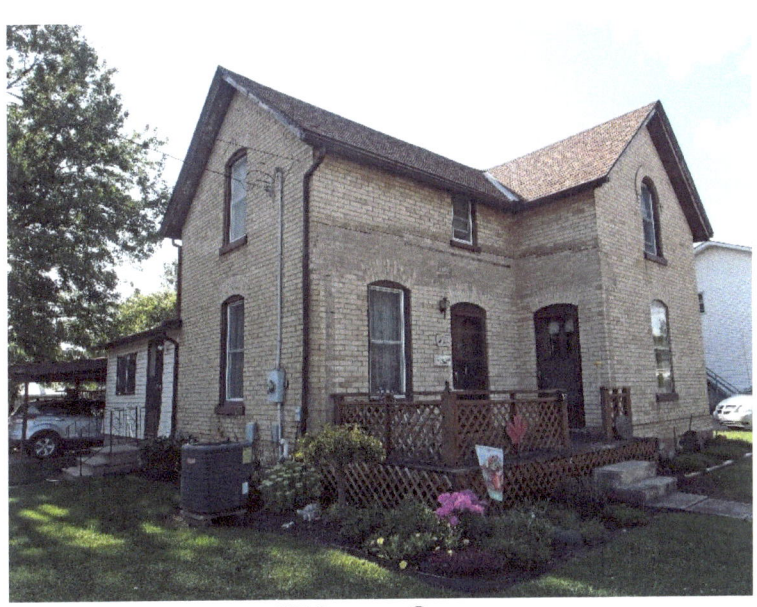

37 Stover Street

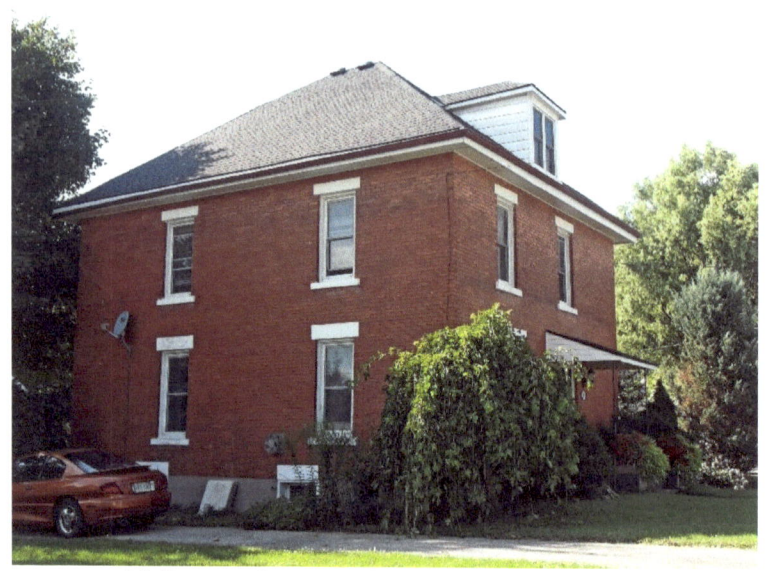

29 Stover Street – hipped roof, dormer

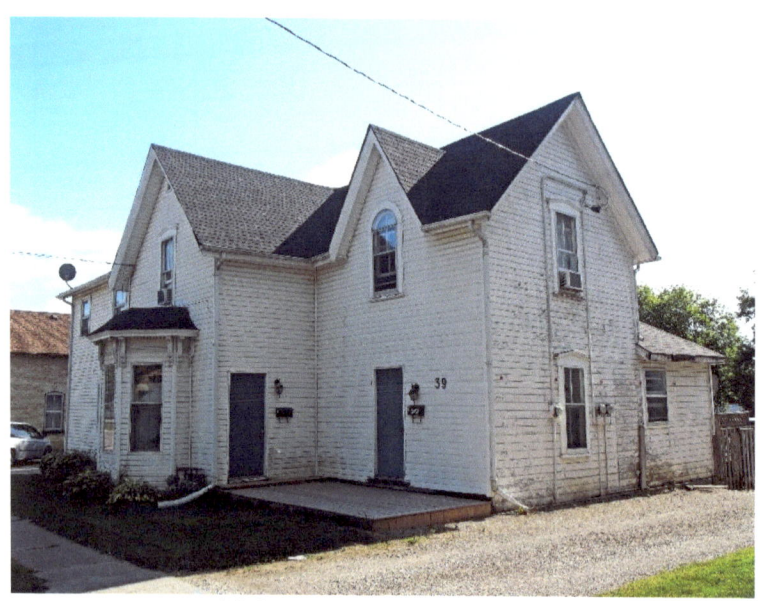

39 Stover Street - Gothic

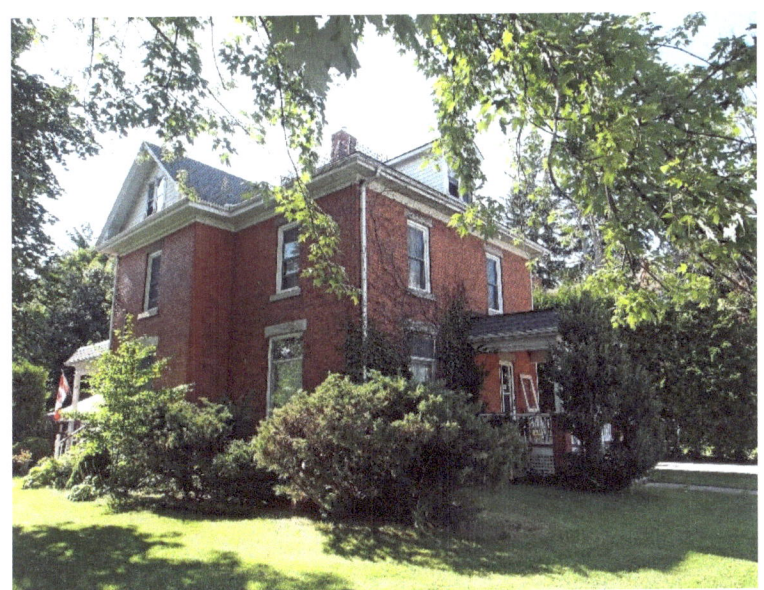

45 Stover Street

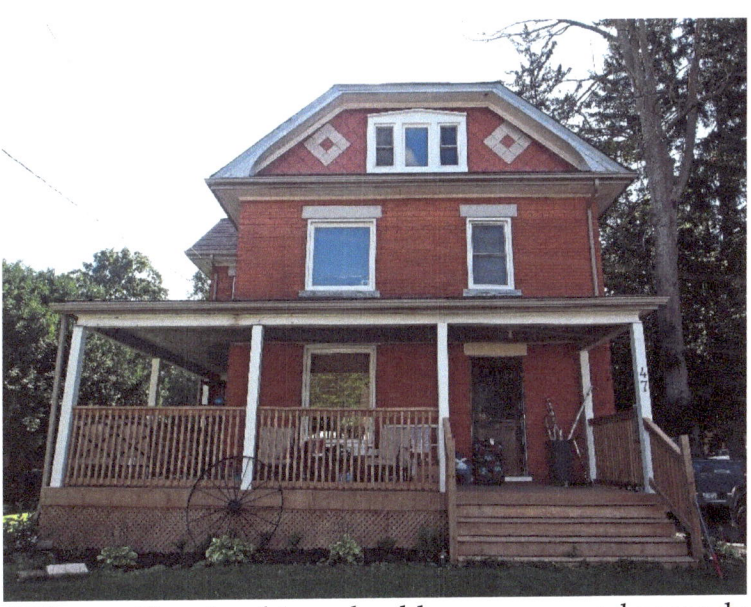

47 Stover Street – chipped gable, wraparound veranda

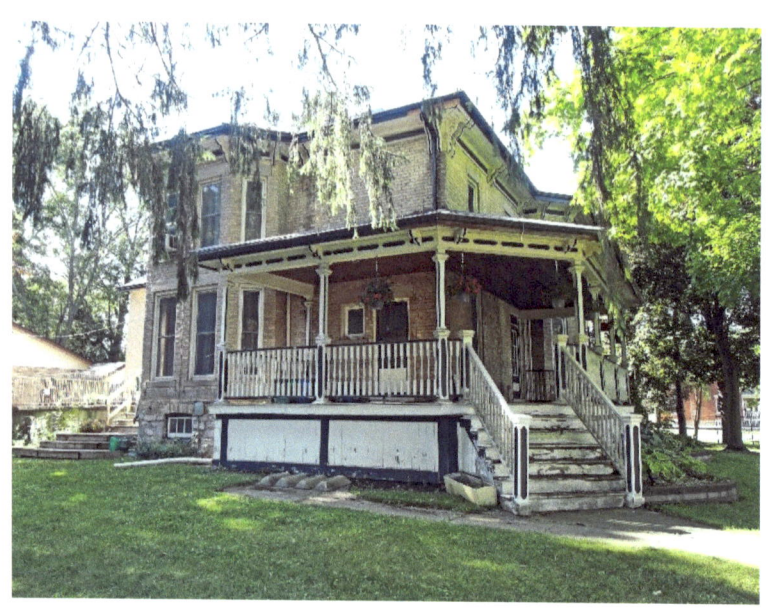

55 Stover Street – wraparound veranda, paired cornice brackets, decorative cornice, bay windows

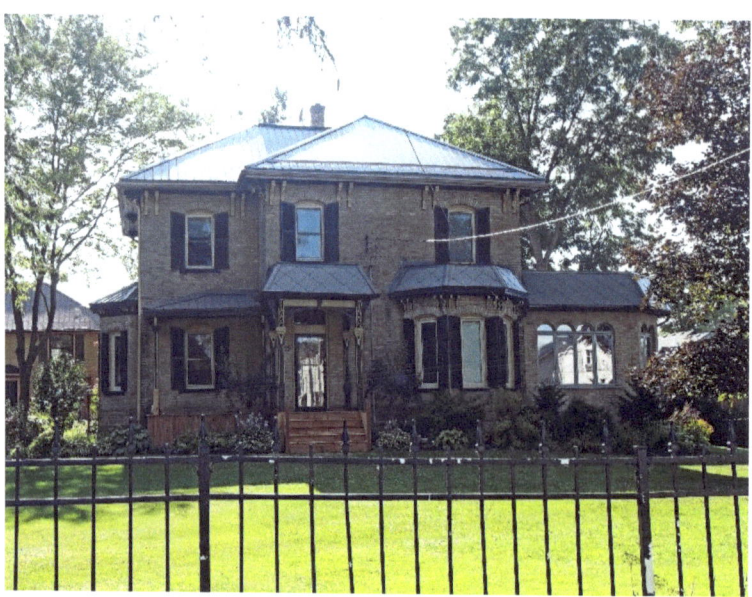

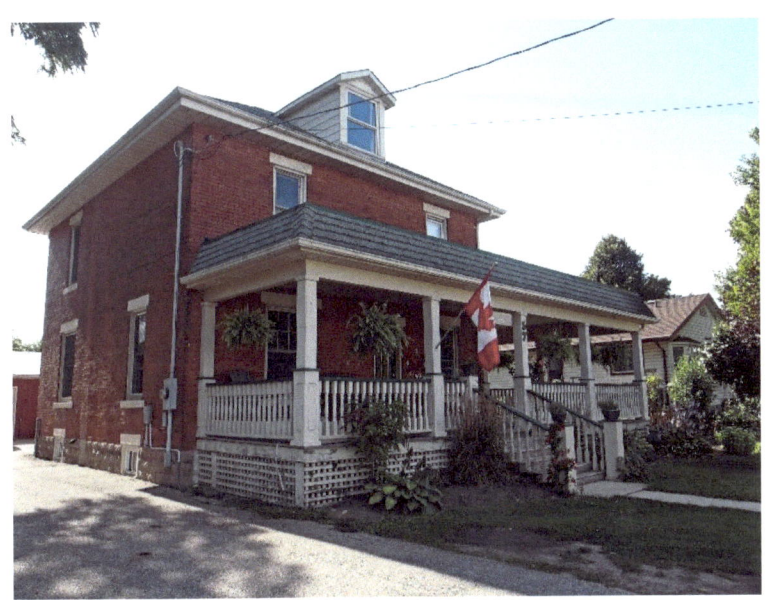

57 Stover Street - dormer

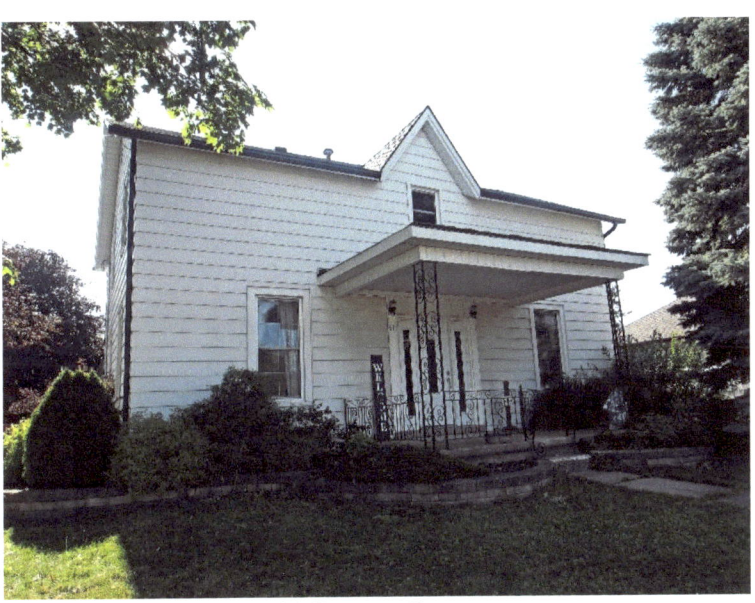

61 Stover Street

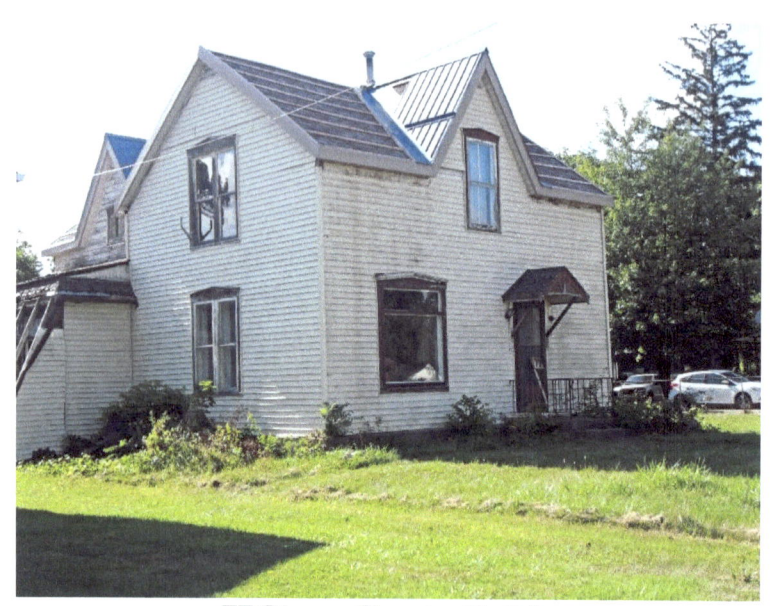

77 Stover Street - Gothic

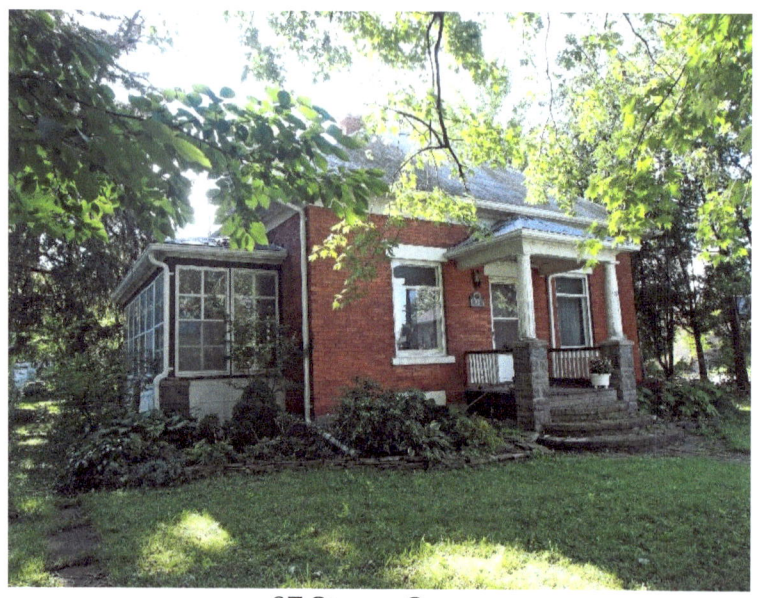

87 Stover Street

The Norwich and District Museum

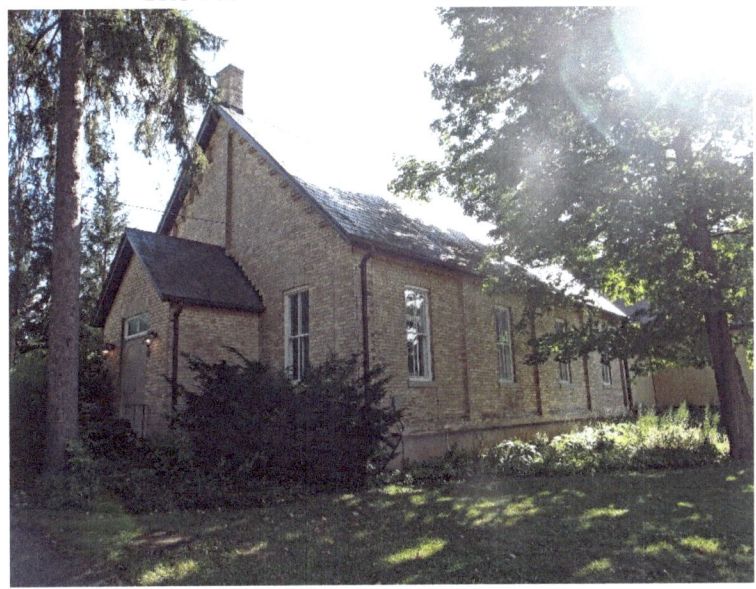

89 Stover Street – Quaker Meeting House – 1889 - designated

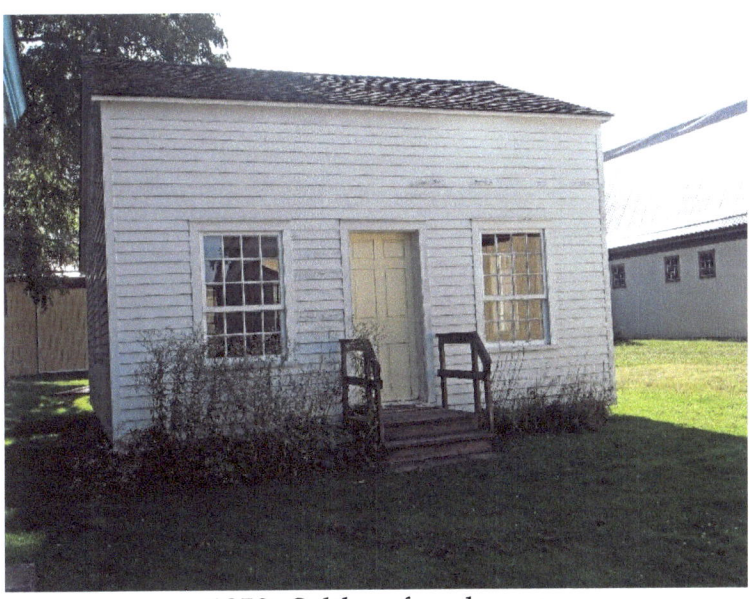

1850s Saltbox farmhouse

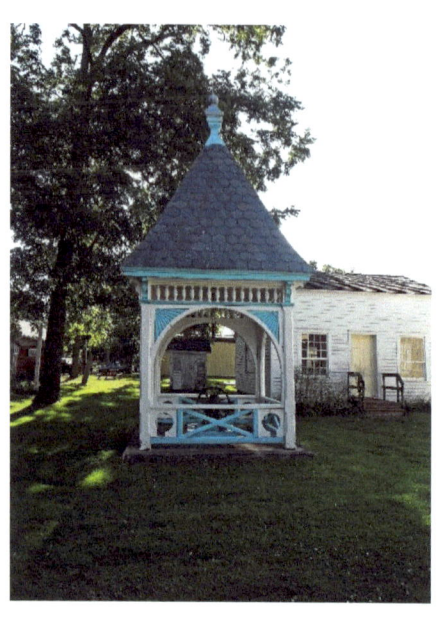

Norwich Public School Belfry 1896-1973

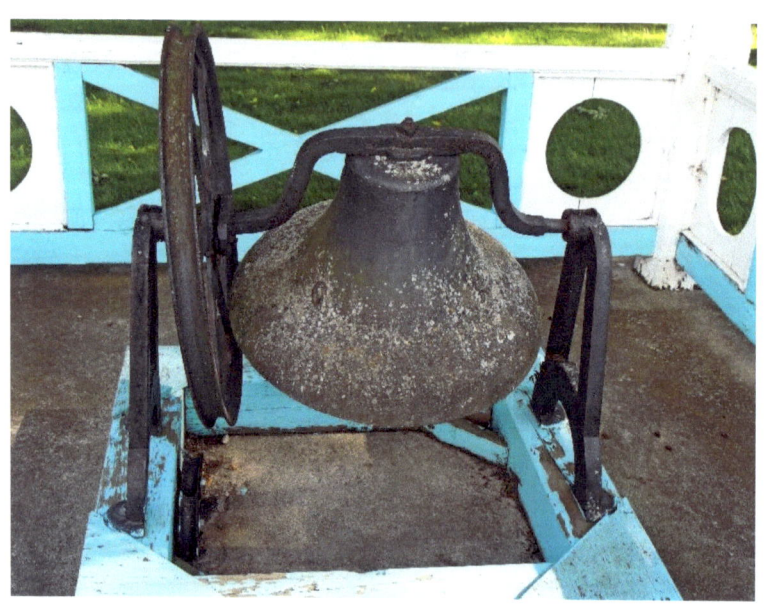

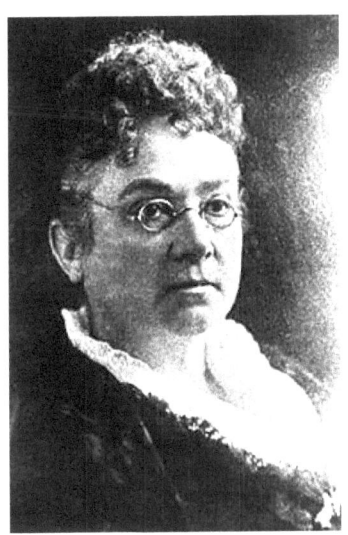

Dr. Emily Howard Stowe

Dr. Emily Howard Stowe was a pioneering Canadian physician and suffragette. She was the first Canadian woman to practice medicine in Canada, and she was a lifelong champion of women's rights. Her tireless campaign to provide women with access to medical schools led to the organization of the women's movement in Canada and to the foundation of a medical college for women.

Emily Howard Jennings was born in 1831 on a farm in Norwich Township in Upper Canada (now Ontario), the first of six daughters of a Methodist father and a Quaker mother. Emily's mother had been well-educated at an American Quaker seminary and believed in a good education for her daughters. She was dissatisfied with the local schools and she chose to instruct all her children herself.

At age 15, Emily became a teacher in a one-room schoolhouse in Summerville where she taught for seven years. In 1852 she applied for admission to Victoria College in Cobourg, but was refused because she was female. She was accepted by Toronto's Normal School for Upper Canada, the only advanced school open to women in British North America. She graduated with first-class honors in 1854.

When she was offered a position with the Brantford School Board, she soon became the first woman principal of a public school in Upper Canada. She remained in the job until her marriage to John Stowe, a native of Yorkshire, England, in 1856. The couple moved to his family's village of Pleasantville, near Brantford, where, over the next seven years, Emily Stowe gave birth to three children. Soon after the birth of John and Emily Stowe's third child, John contracted tuberculosis. His illness inspired Emily to explore the field of herbal healing and homeopathic medicine, an area her mother had studied. This, together with what she saw as a serious need for women doctors, led to her decision to become a physician.

In 1865, Emily Stowe applied to the Toronto School of Medicine, but once again, she was denied admission – no women allowed.

Unable to study in Canada, she moved to the United States and enrolled at the New York Medical College for Women, a homeopathic institution in the city of New York. She obtained her degree in 1867 and returned to Canada and set up a practice in homeopathic medicine on Richmond Street in Toronto, even before obtaining her license. She was the first practicing female physician in Canada.

It was not until 1871 that Dr. Stowe and Jenny Trout, another aspiring doctor, were finally admitted to the school, and even then, only by special arrangement. They were thus the first two women to attend lectures at the Toronto School of Medicine. Dr. Stowe continued her medical practice, specializing in women and children and giving lectures on women's health.

John Stowe died in 1891 and Emily Stowe 12 years later, in 1903. It was another fourteen years before women got the vote in Canada and much of the credit goes to Dr. Emily Stowe, teacher, physician and passionate suffragist.

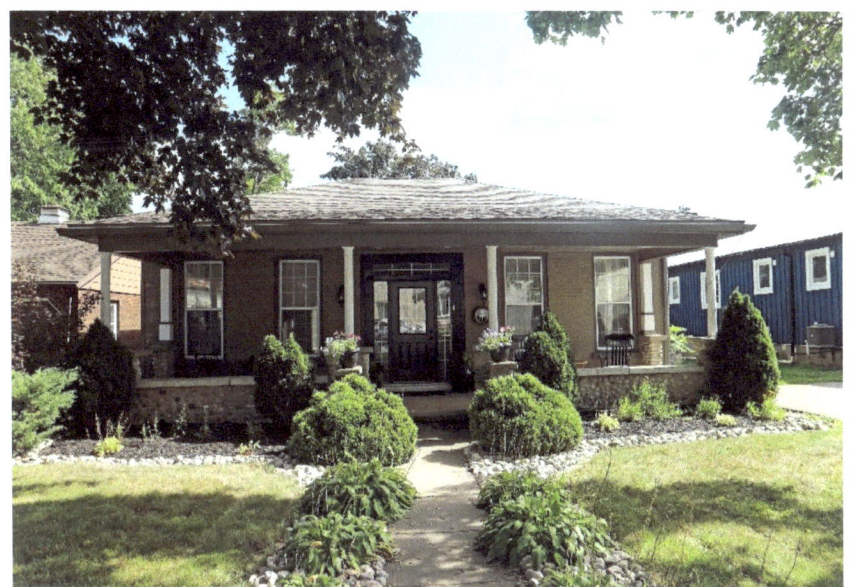

4 Main Street East – Regency Cottage, hipped roof

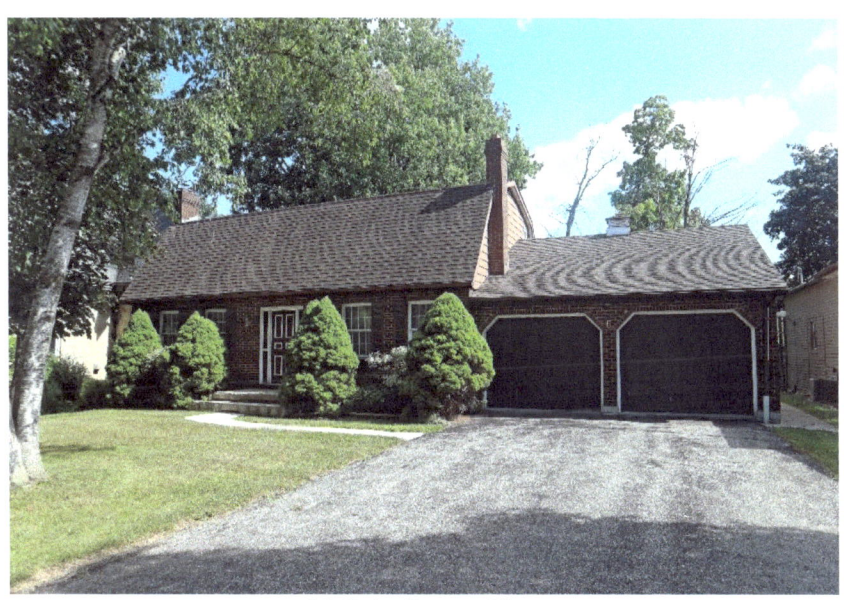

6 Main Street East

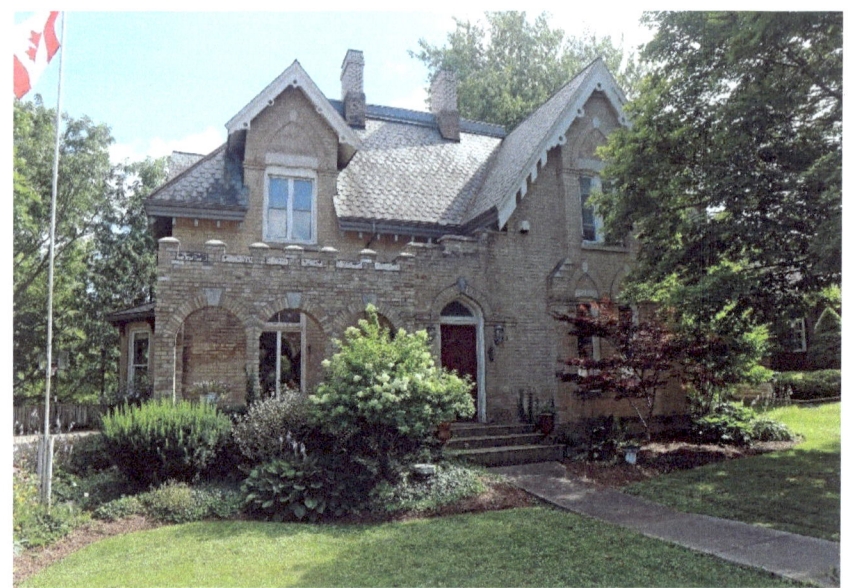

8 Main Street East – designated – Moore, Chambers House – Gothic, verge board trim on gables, crenelated brick arched veranda with voussoirs and keystones, bay window on side, transom above door

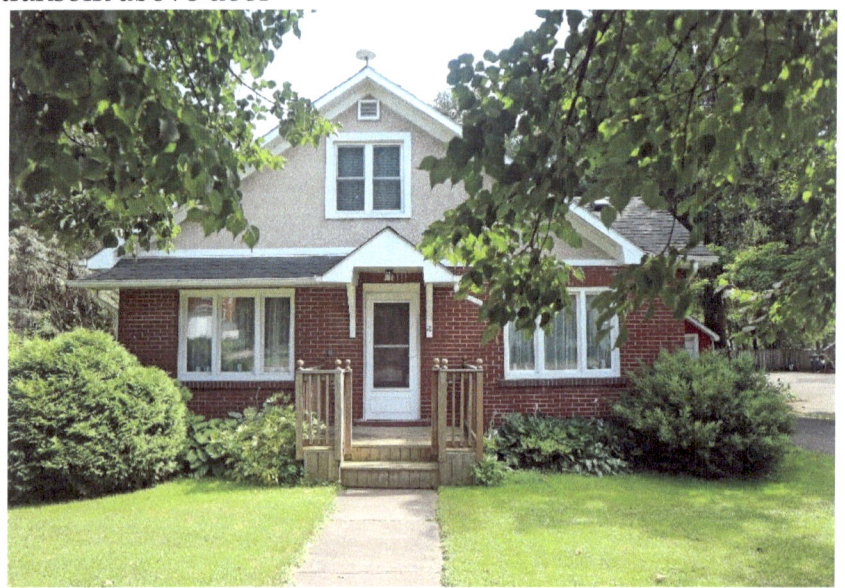

10 Main Street East

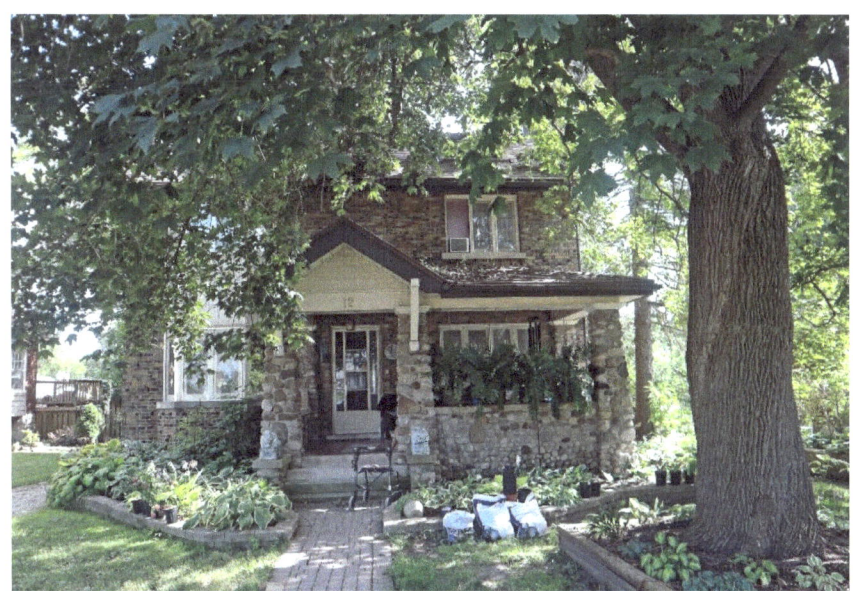

12 Main Street East – cobblestone pillars and veranda

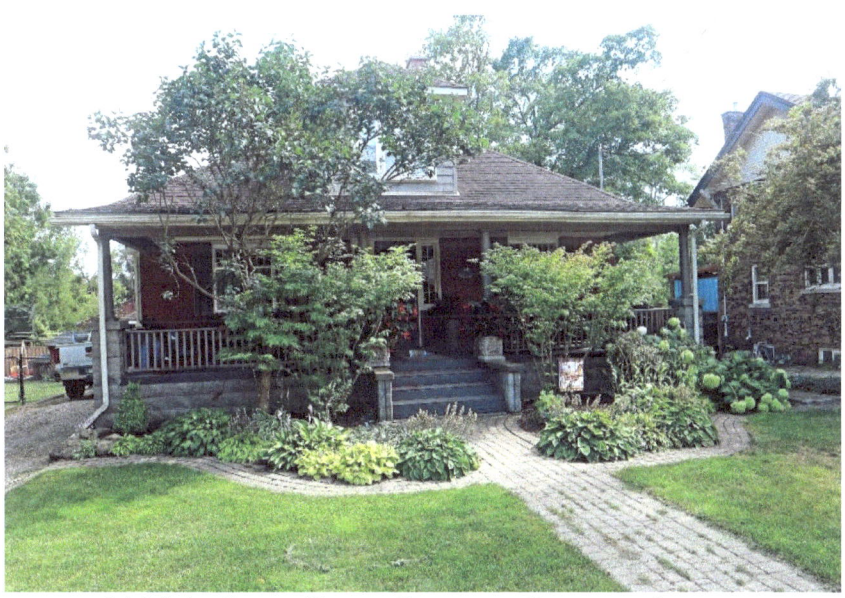

14 Main Street East – Regency Cottage, dormer

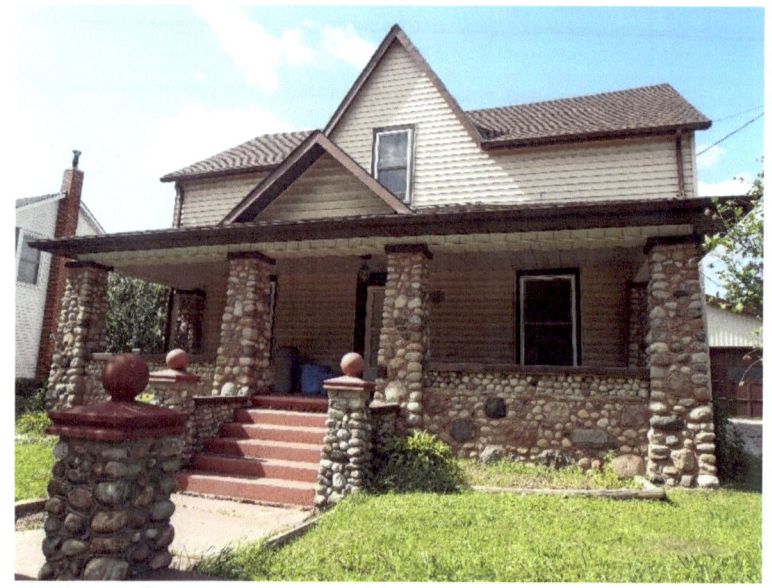

15 Main Street East – cobblestone pillars and veranda

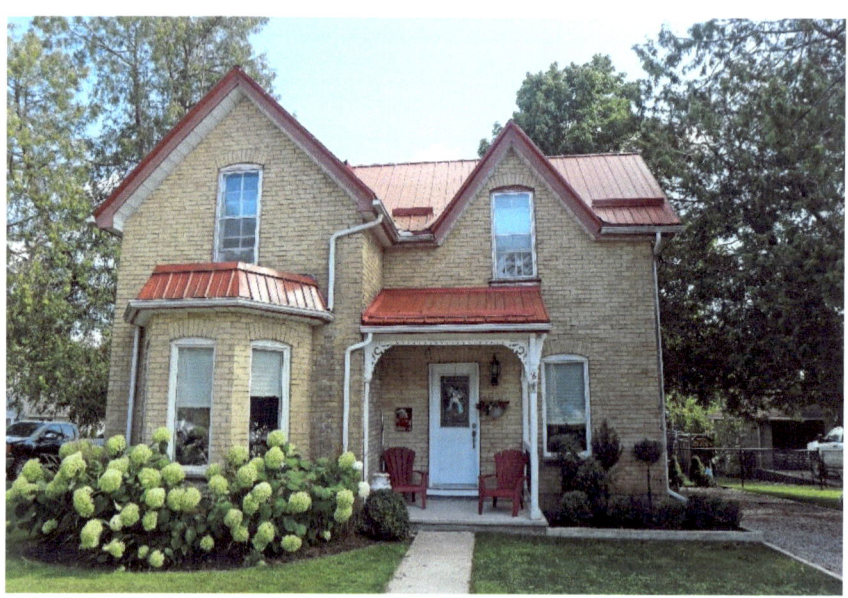

16 Main Street East – Gothic – bay window

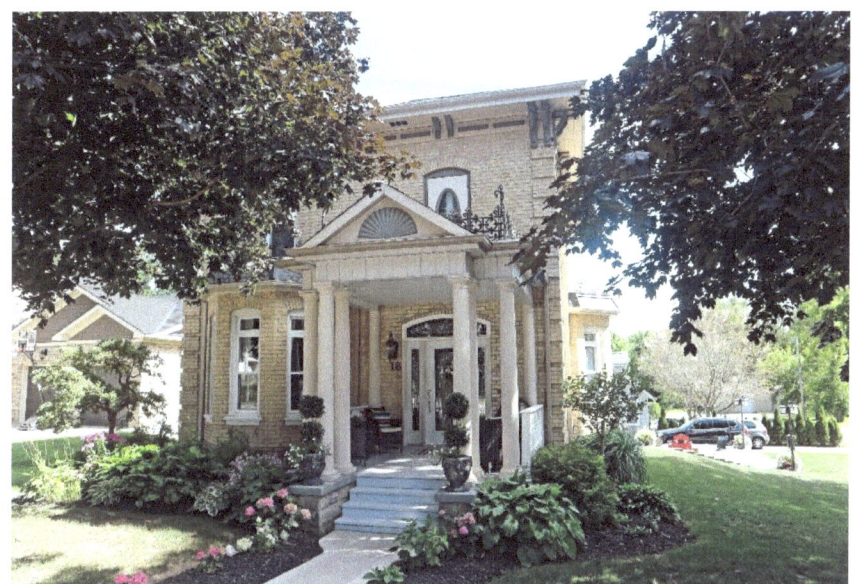

18 Main Street East – Italianate, paired cornice brackets, decorative cornice, corner quoins, pediment with decorated tympanum above Doric pillars, sidelights and transom surround door, bay window on front and side

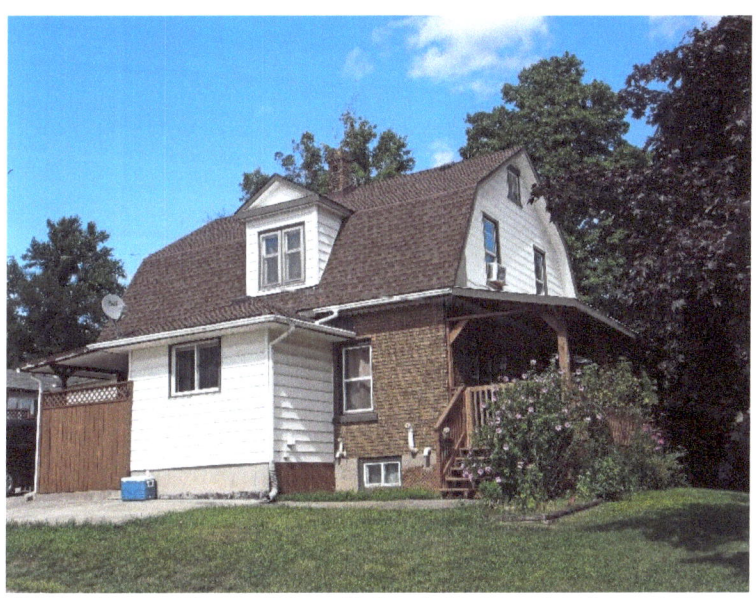

19 Main Street East – Neo-Colonial – gambrel roof, dormer

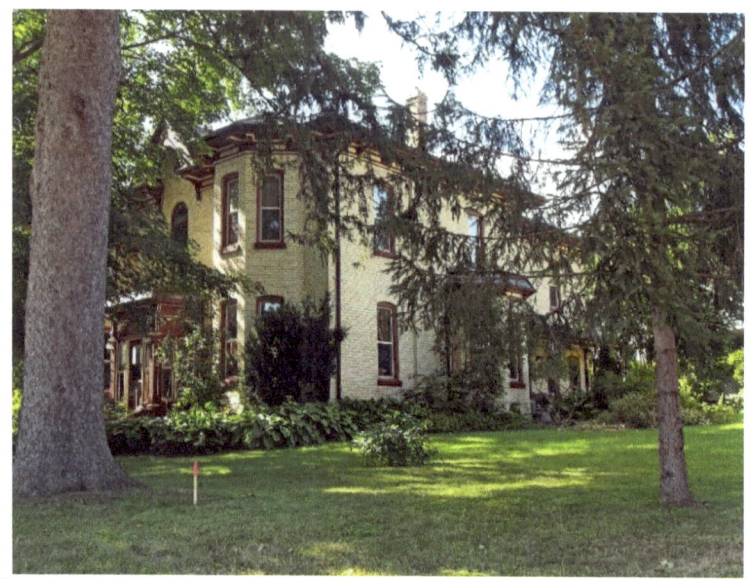

23 Main Street East - The plan of this elegant two and a half storey house is rectangular, with exterior walls of white clay brick laid in a garden wall design and with a natural cut stone foundation. A wooden frieze below the eaves adds an extra touch of refinement below the low gable roof. This house was originally built in the 1880s for Reverend James Bidwell Freeman.

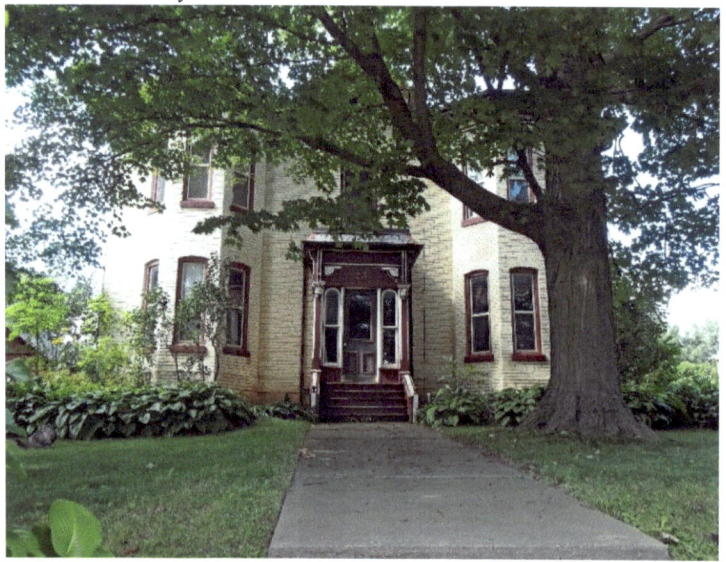

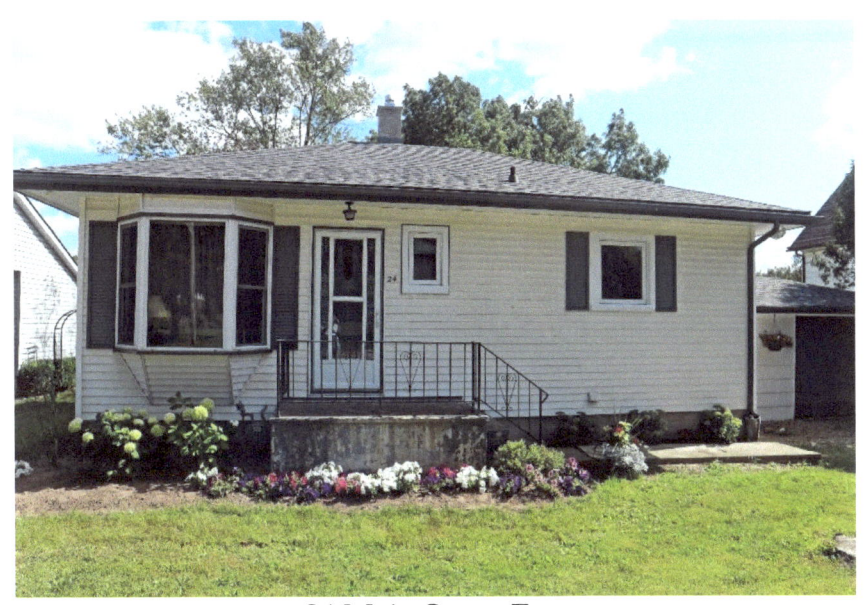

24 Main Street East

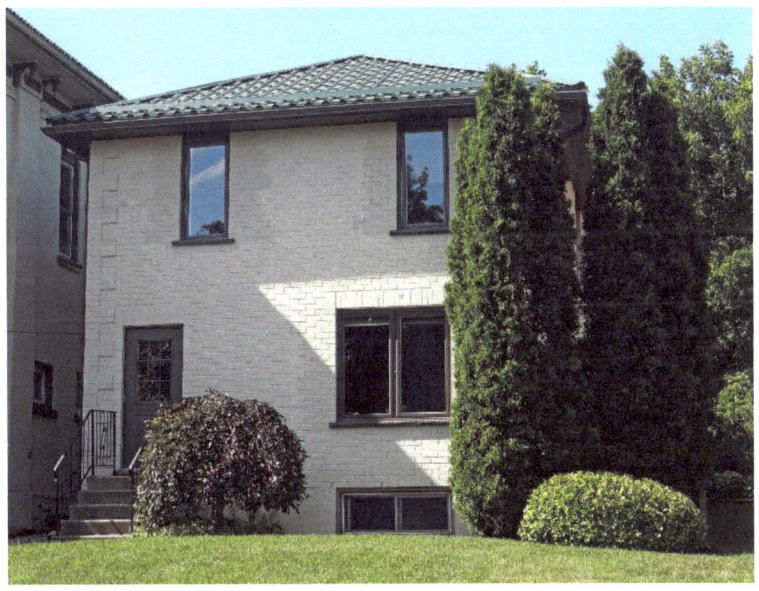

Main Street East

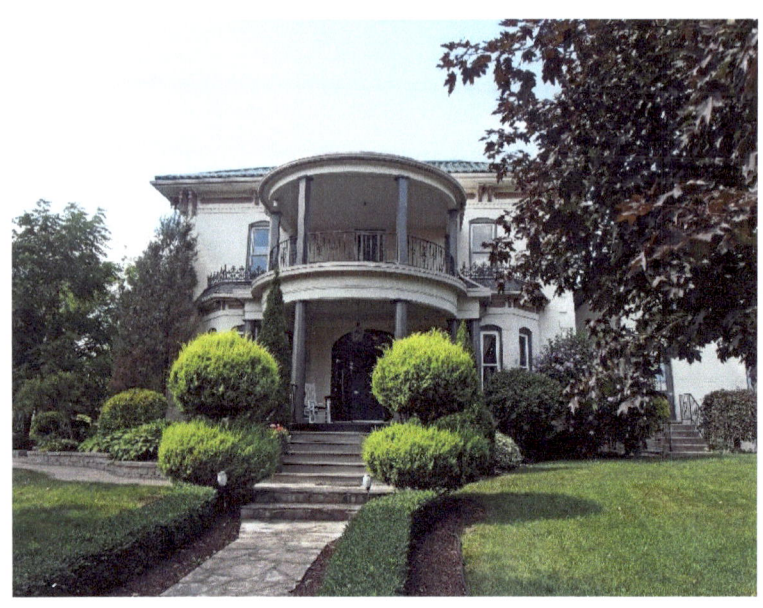

25 Main Street East – Trillium Christian Retirement Home – two-story semi-circular veranda, bay windows, iron cresting, paired cornice brackets, corner quoins

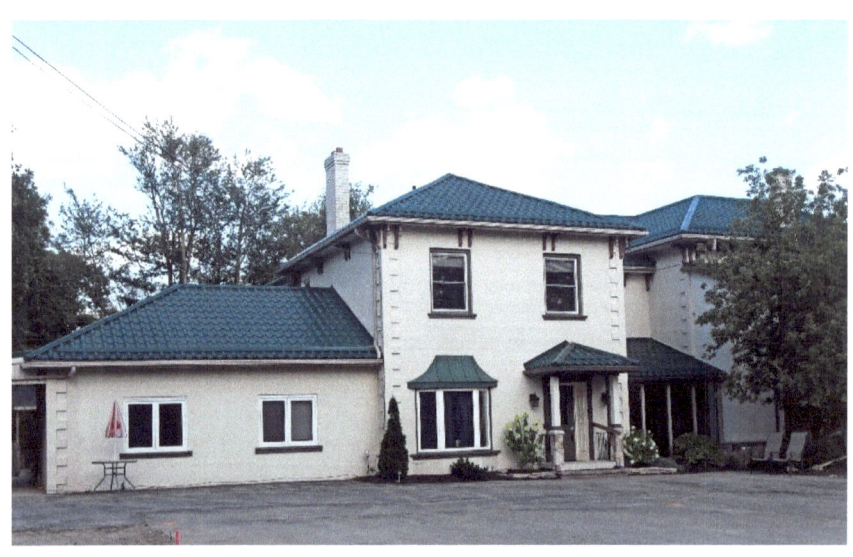

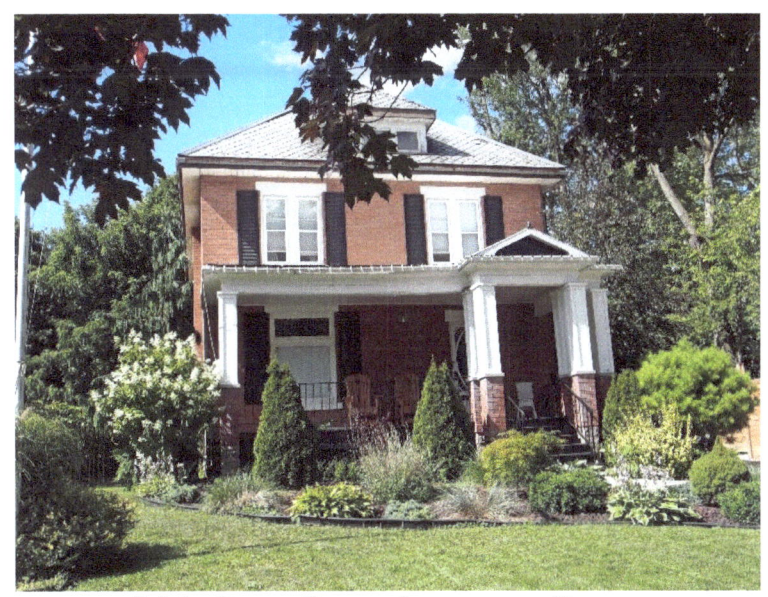

Main Street East – dormer, pediment

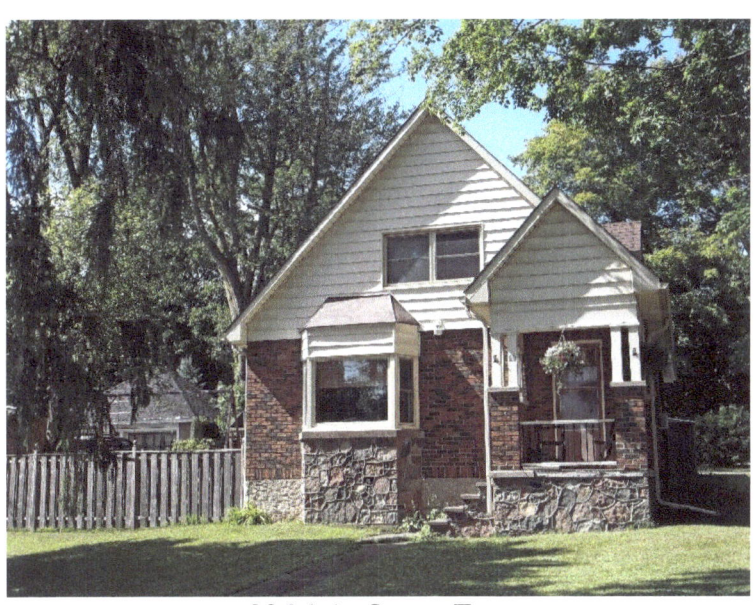

29 Main Street East

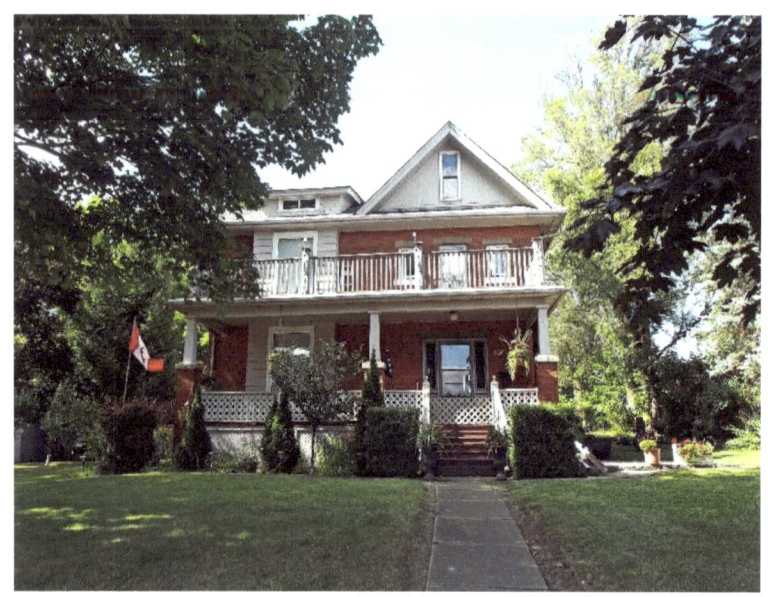

31 Main Street East

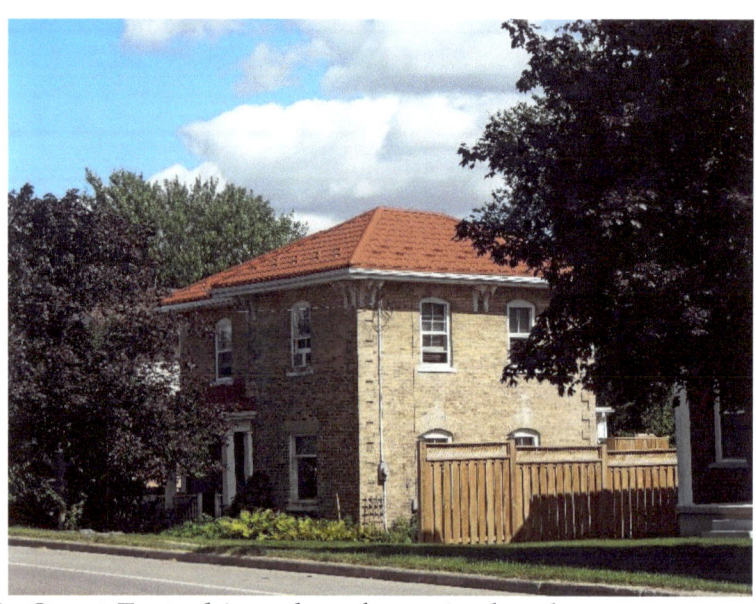

Main Street East – hipped roof, cornice brackets, corner quoins

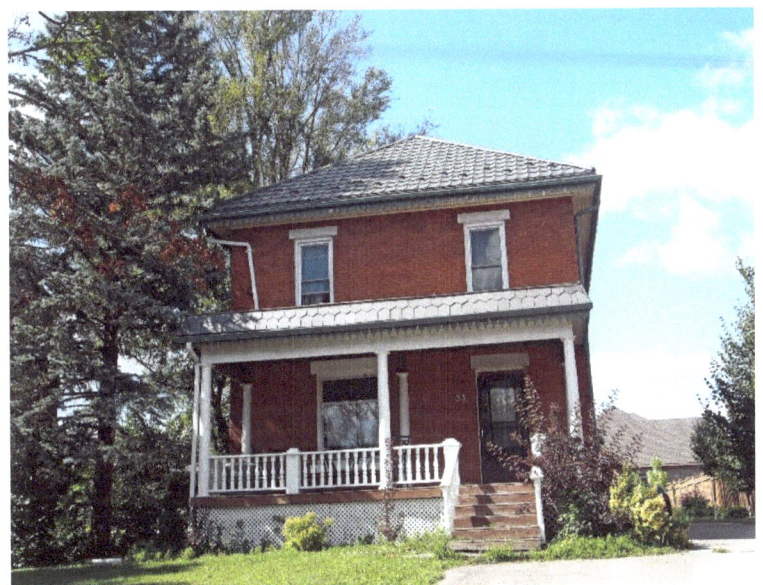

33 Main Street East – hipped roof

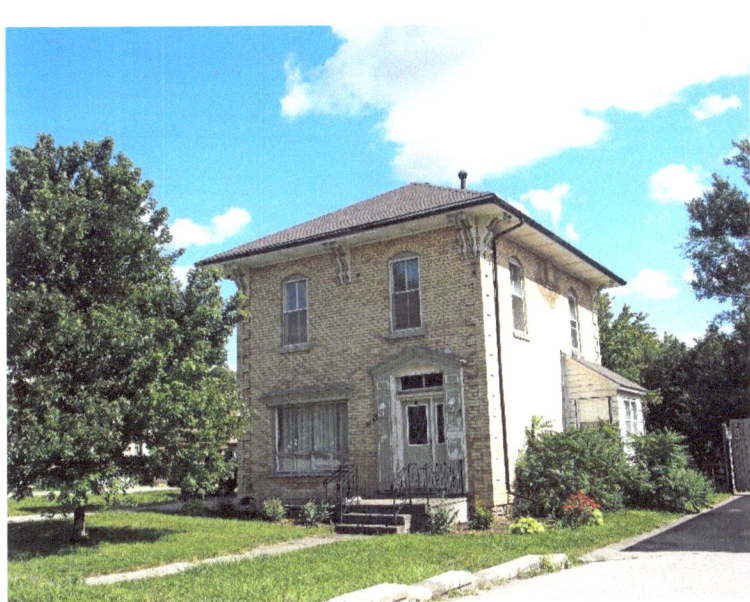

46 Main Street East – Italianate – hipped roof, cornice brackets

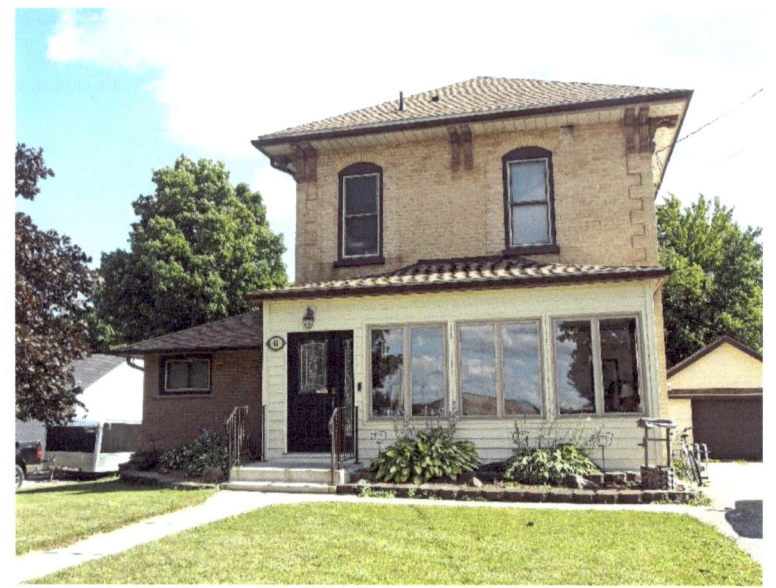

48 Main Street East – paired cornice brackets, corner quoins

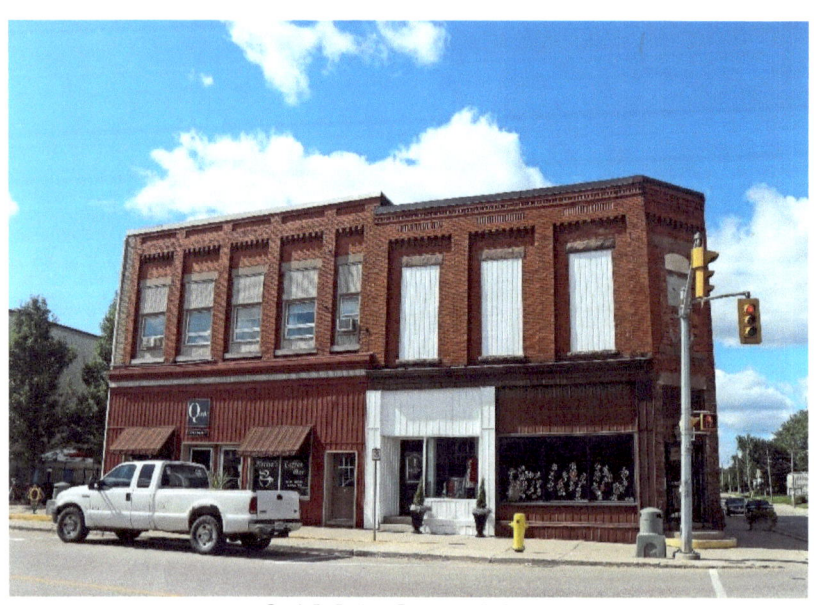

2-4 Main Street West

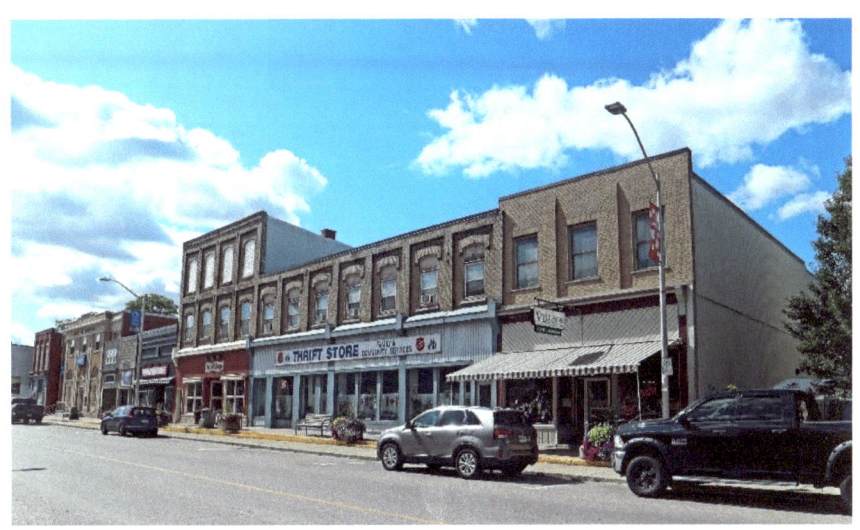

Main Street West

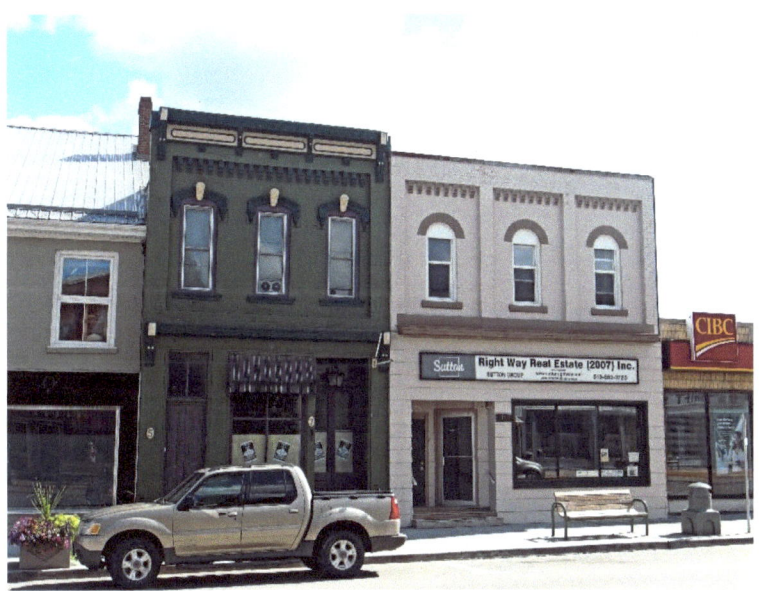

5-11 Main Street West – dentil molding

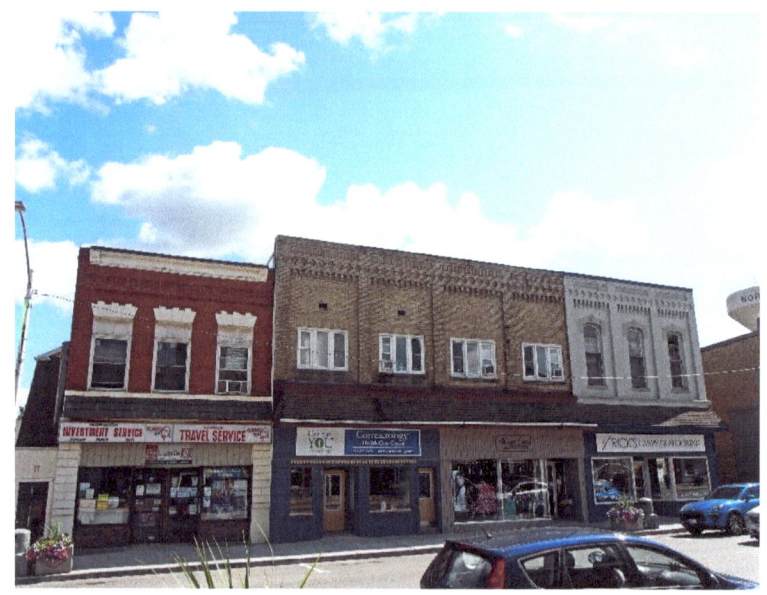

17-23 Main Street West

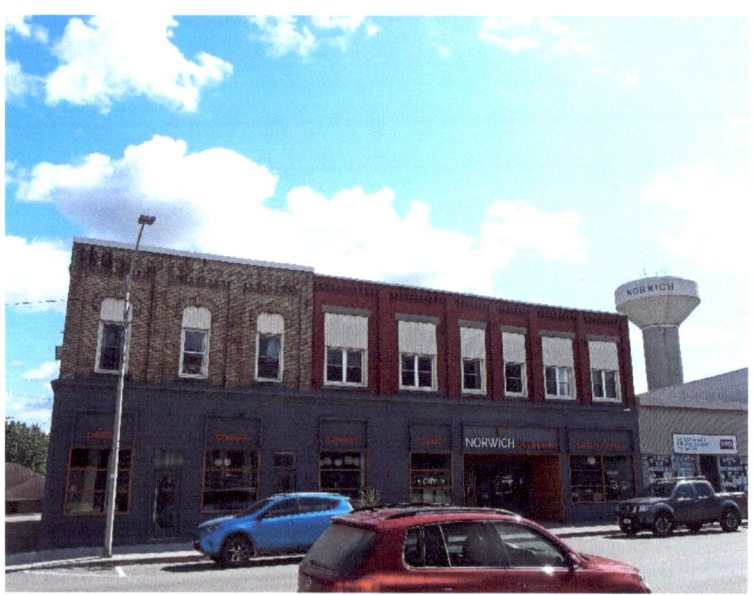

27 Main Street West

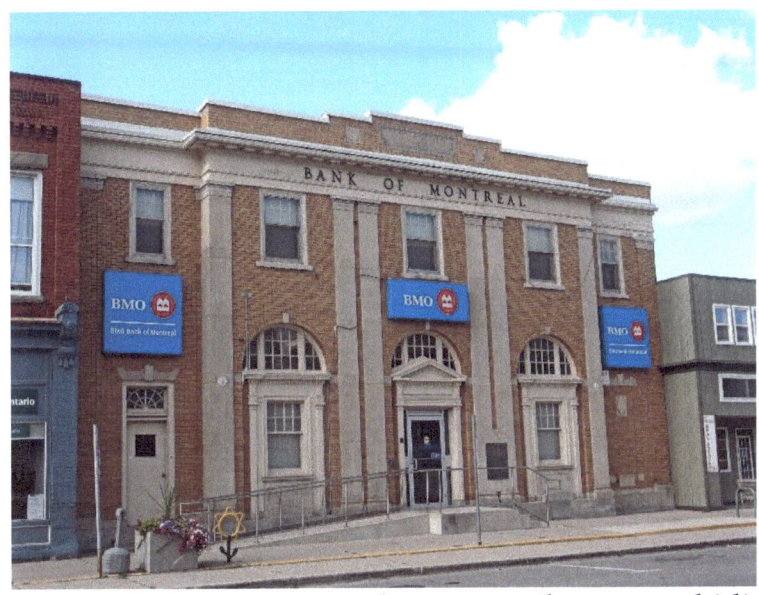

30 Main Street West – stepped parapet, pilasters, multi-light transoms

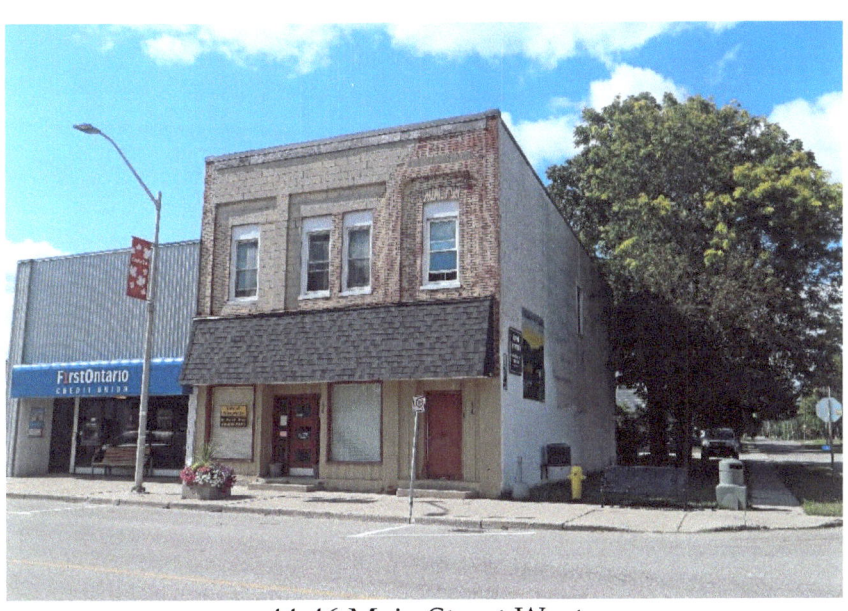

44-46 Main Street West

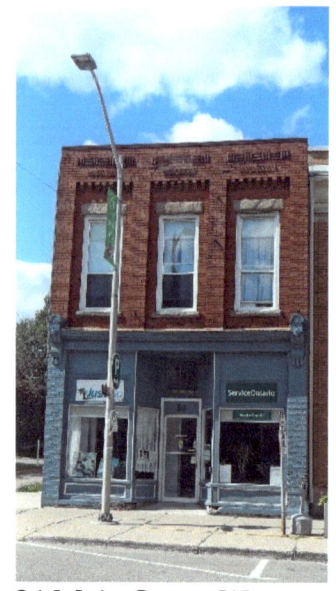 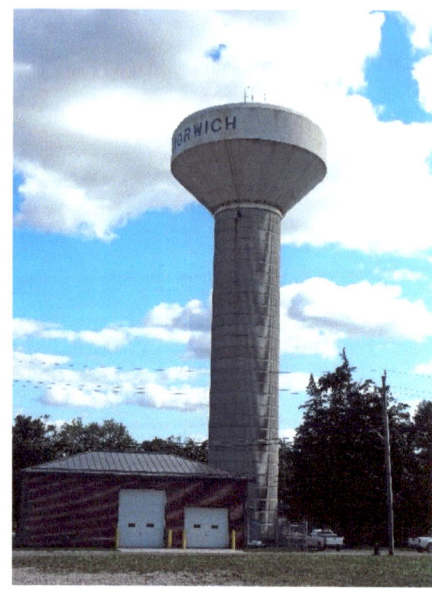

34 Main Street West

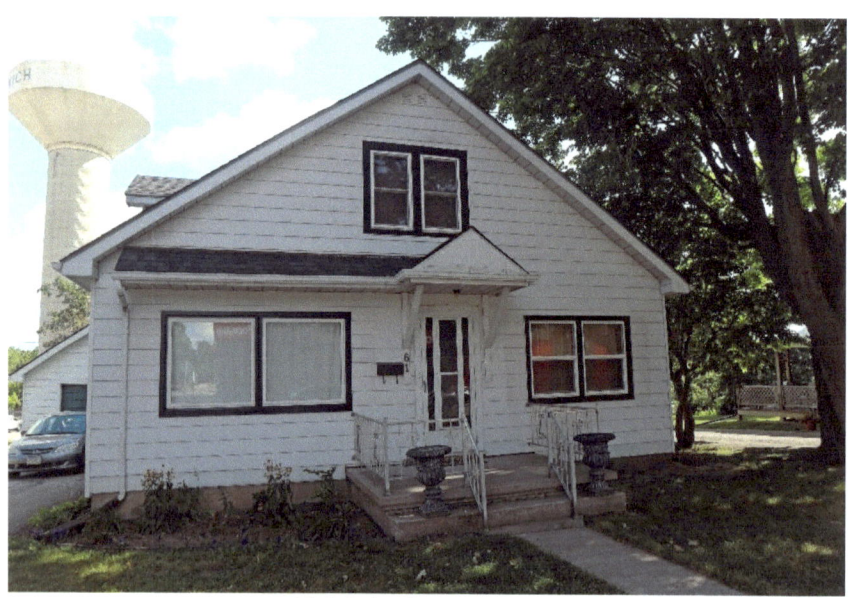

61 Main Street West

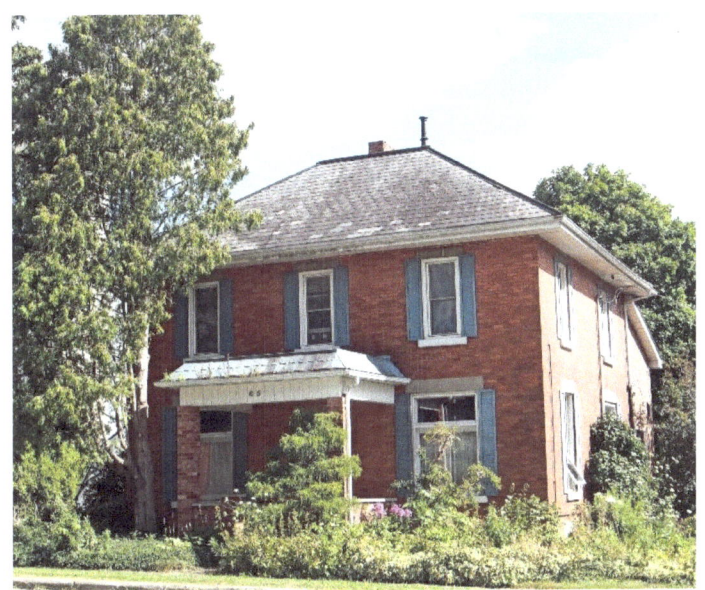

65 Main Street West

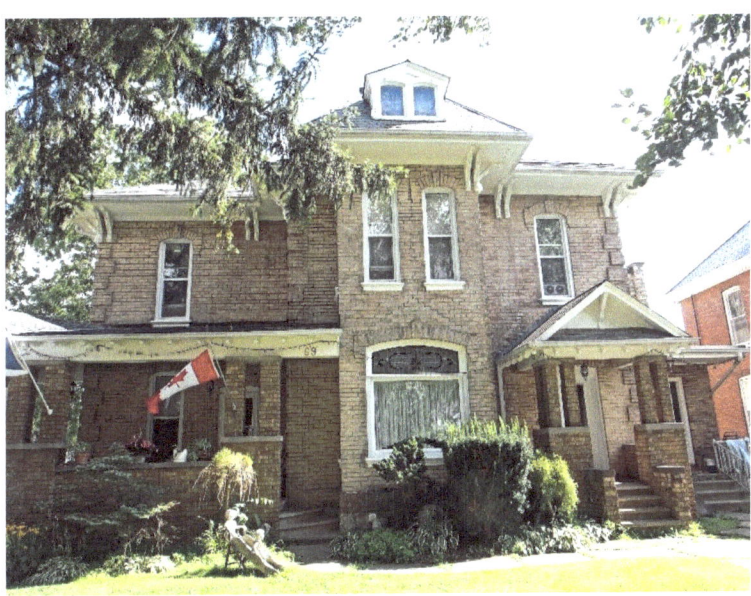

69 Main Street West – Italianate, dormer, paired cornice brackets, corner quoins, pediment

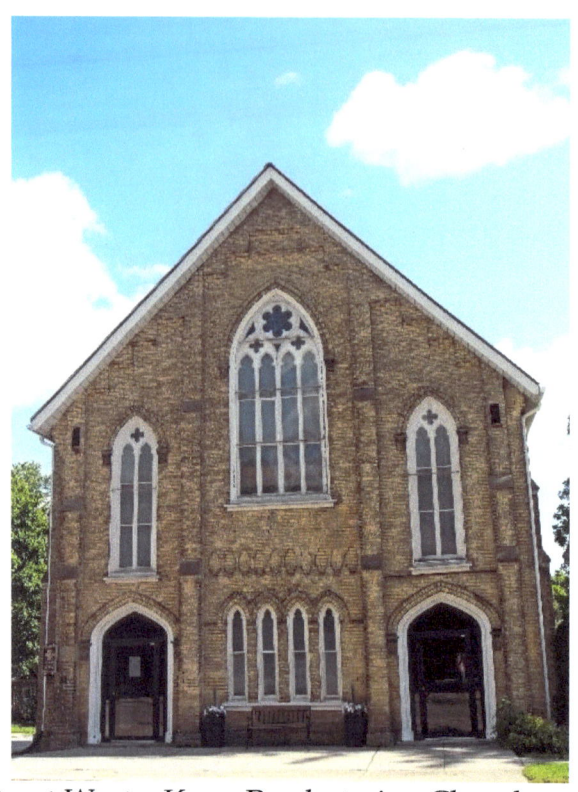

67 Main Street West – Knox Presbyterian Church – two-storey white-clay brick church constructed in 1879, Gothic Revival – steeply pitched gable roof and lancet arched windows and entrances, buttresses, elaborate central window on façade formed by a pair of double trefoil lancet windows surmounted by a coloured glass surround, and the double trefoil lancet windows on the façade and side elevations, capped with a cruciform window of coloured glass and a brick surround. The double main entrances have elaborate wood and brick surrounds that incorporate a roped design labelled with relief carvings of wooden leaf motifs.

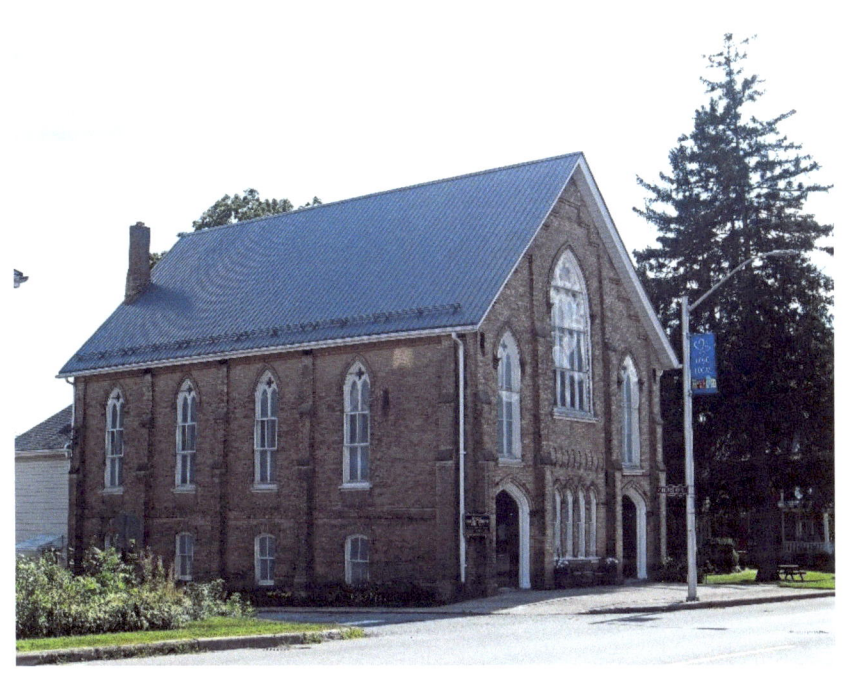

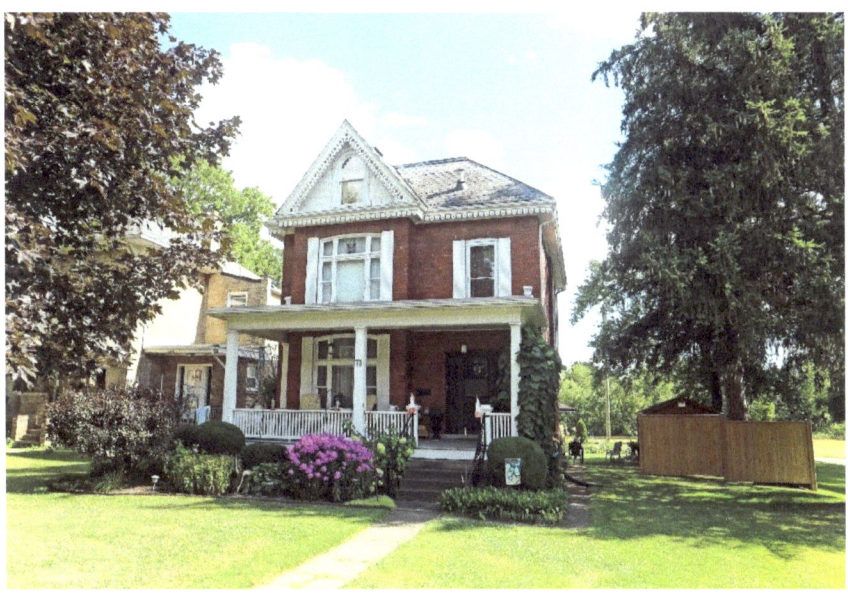

73 Main Street West

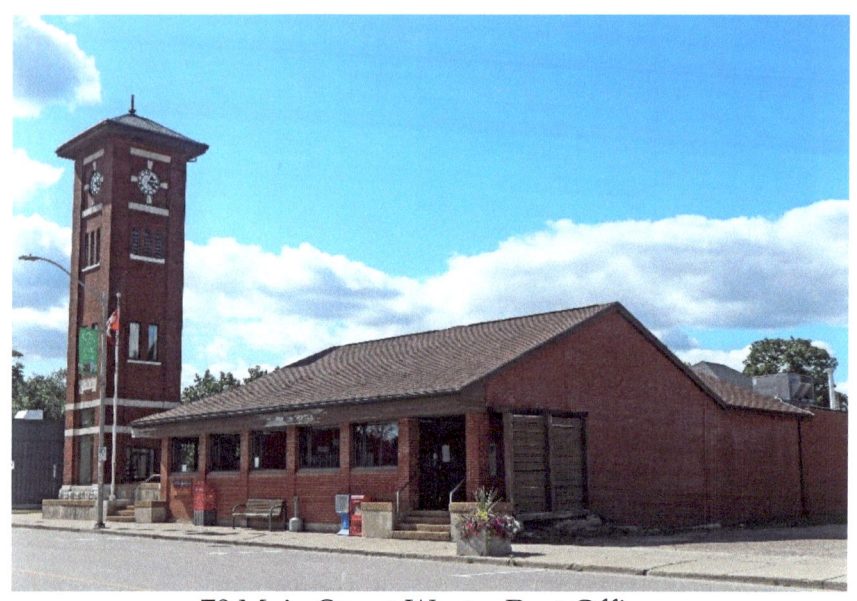

70 Main Street West – Post Office

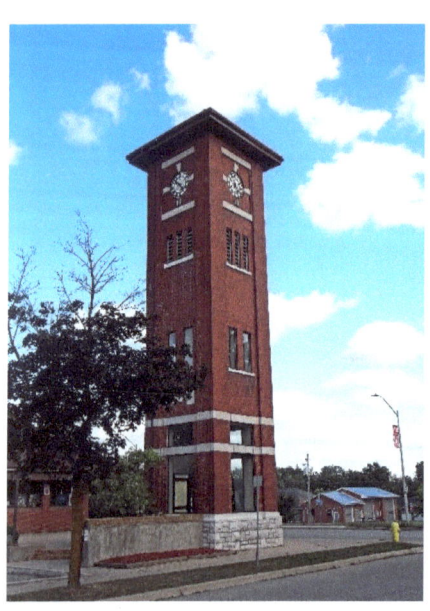
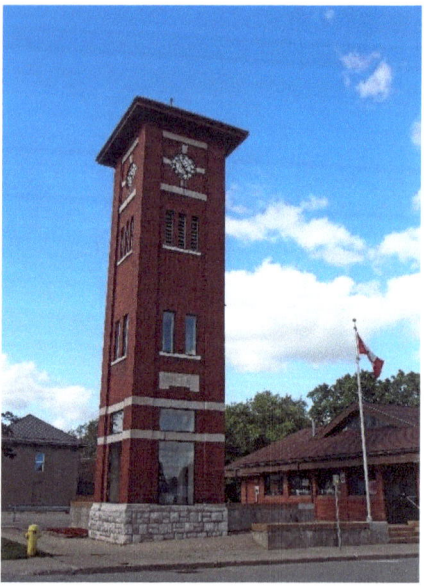

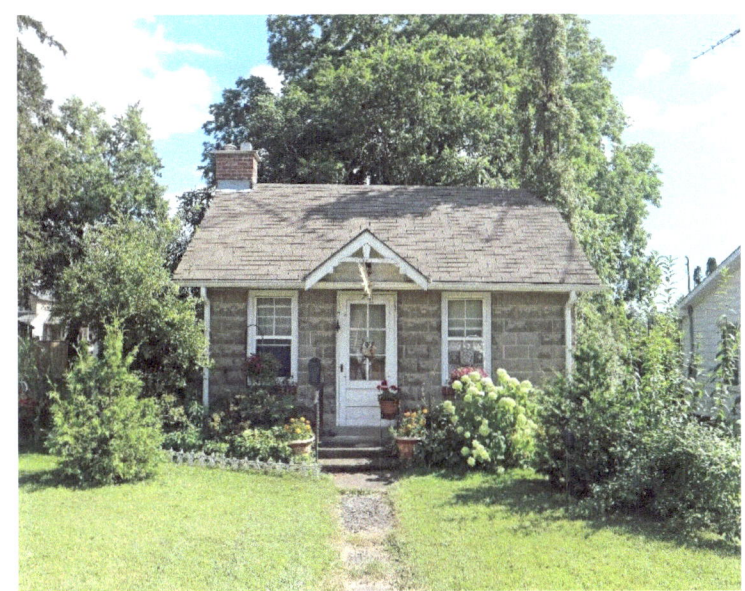

75 Main Street West

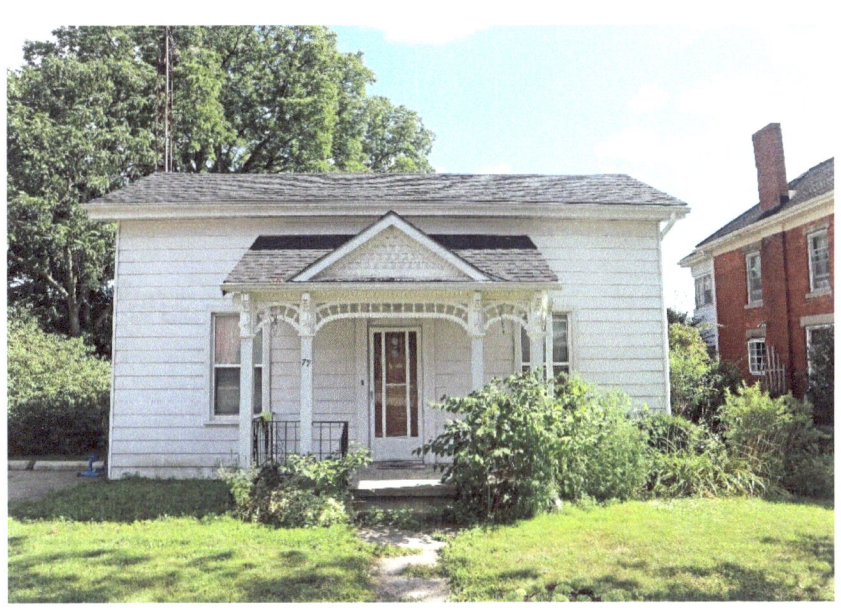

77 Main Street West

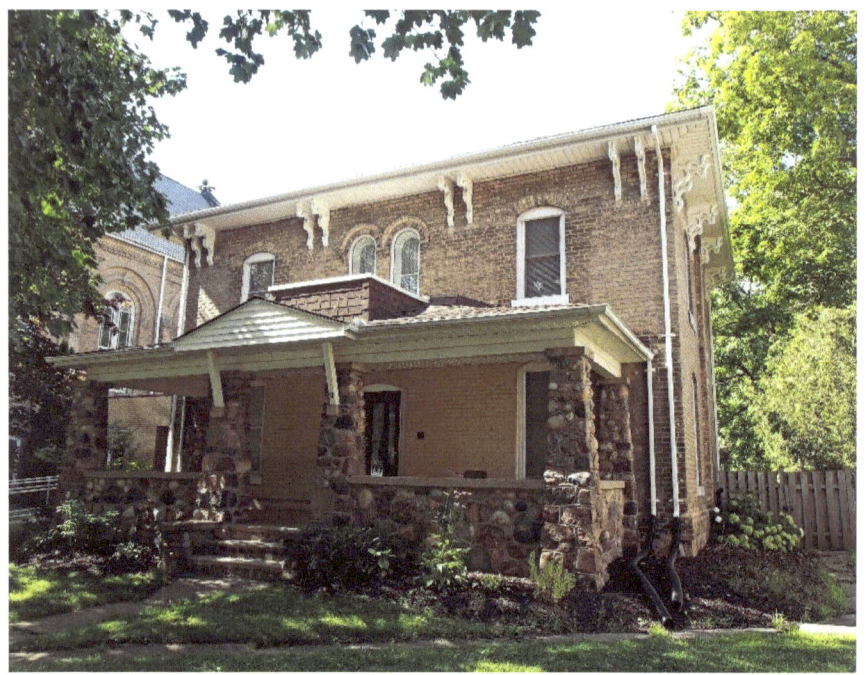

78 Main Street West - Norwich United Church Manse – two-storey white-brick manse was constructed in 1875 – a blocky, Italianate residence with symmetry of paired cornice brackets and twin round-headed windows and doors of second-storey

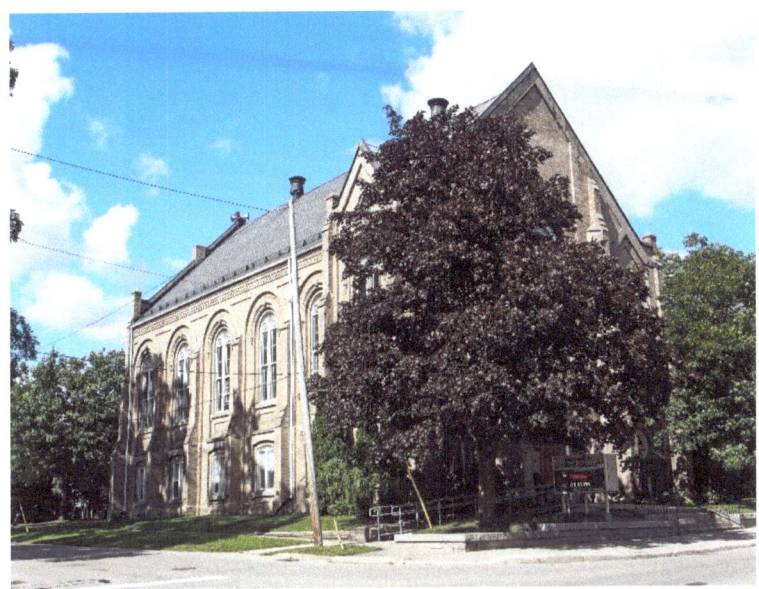

80 Main Street West – Norwich United Church – 1885 (Methodist Church) – designated – Italianate - broad gable with three recessed doors below triple round-headed windows, slender buttresses which grow out of the bases of the molded window surrounds

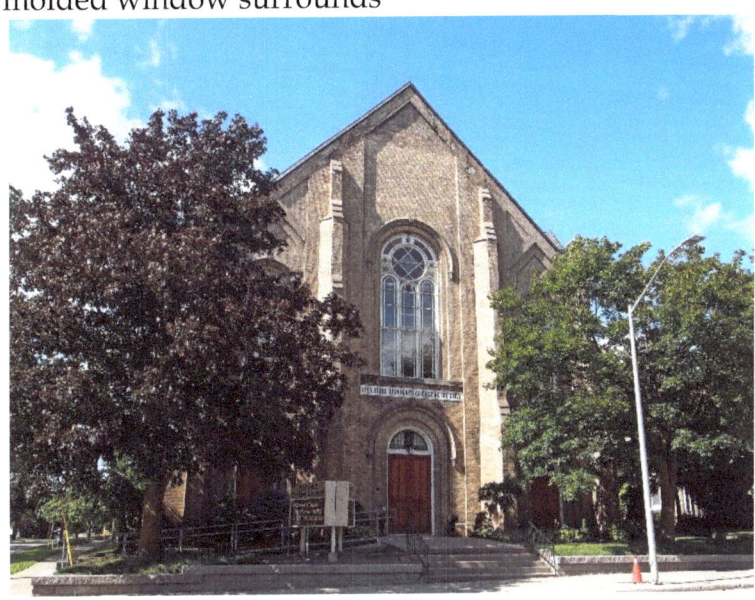

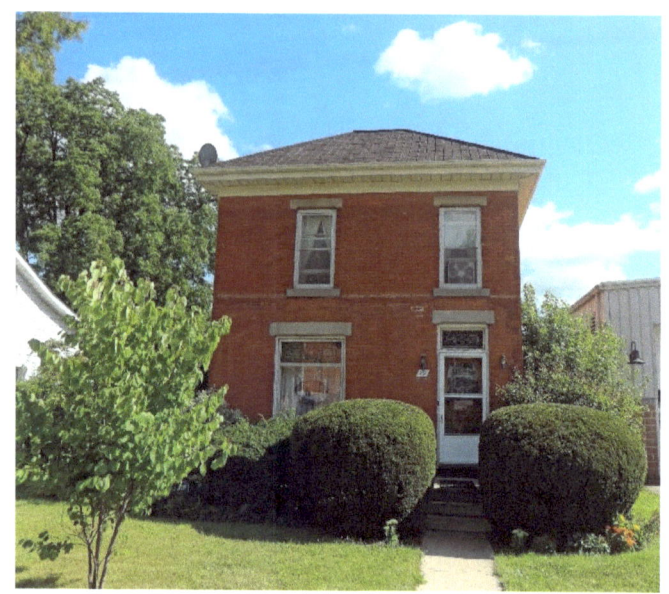
79 Main Street West - banding

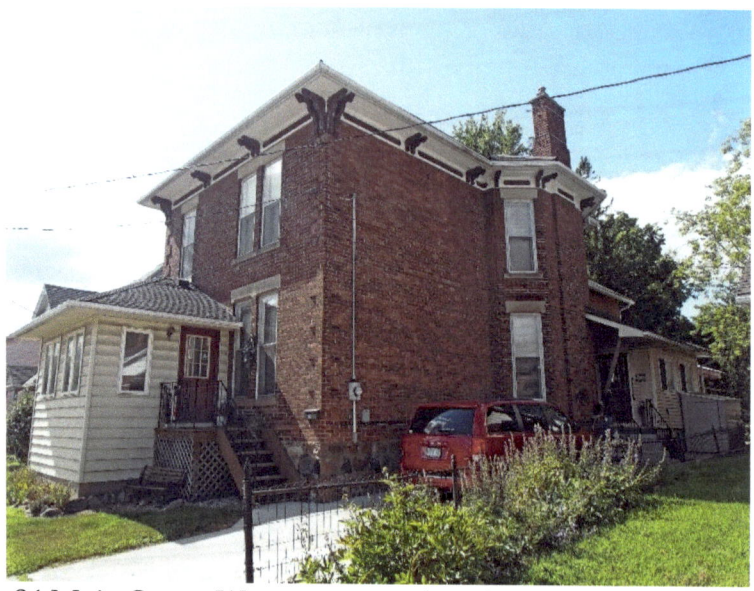
84 Main Street West – cornice brackets, corner quoins

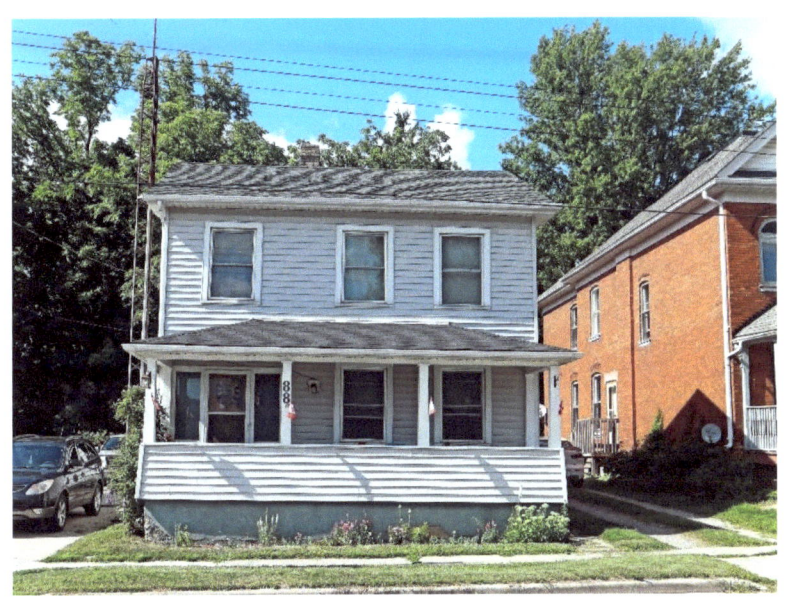

88 Main Street West

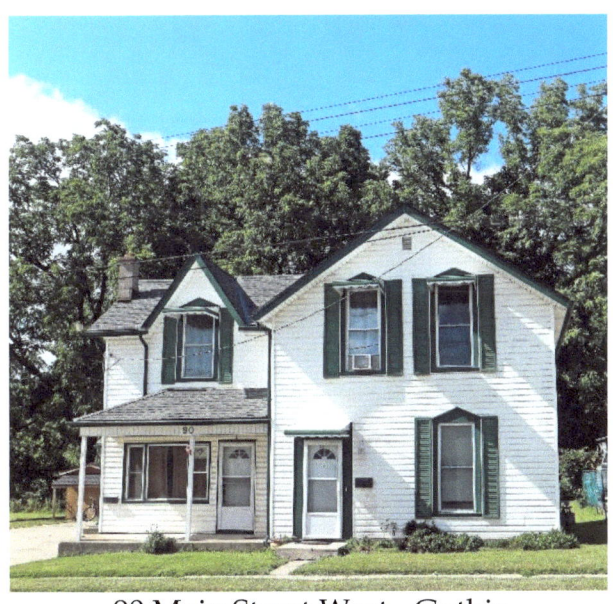

90 Main Street West - Gothic

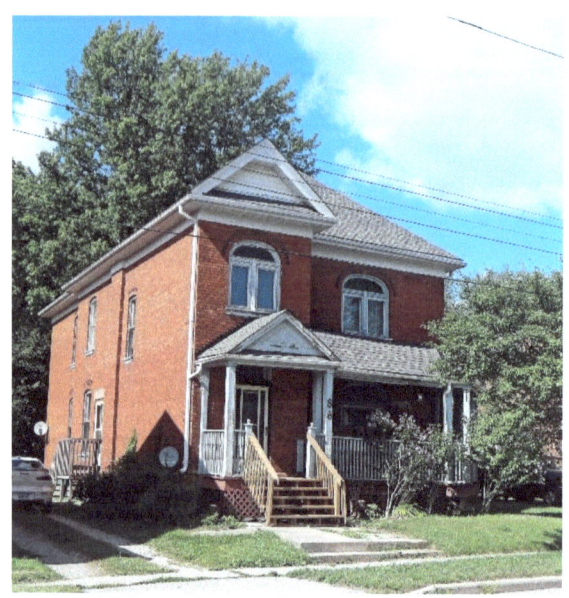

86 Main Street West - pediment

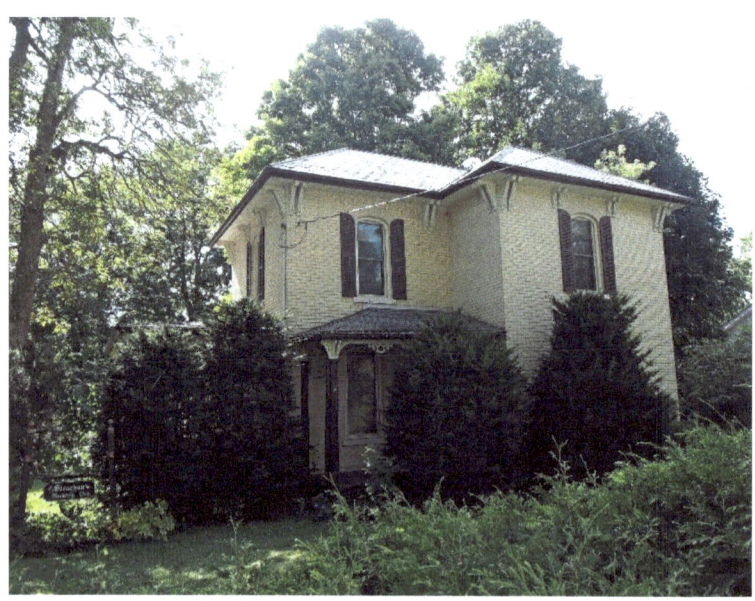

3 Clyde Street – cornice brackets

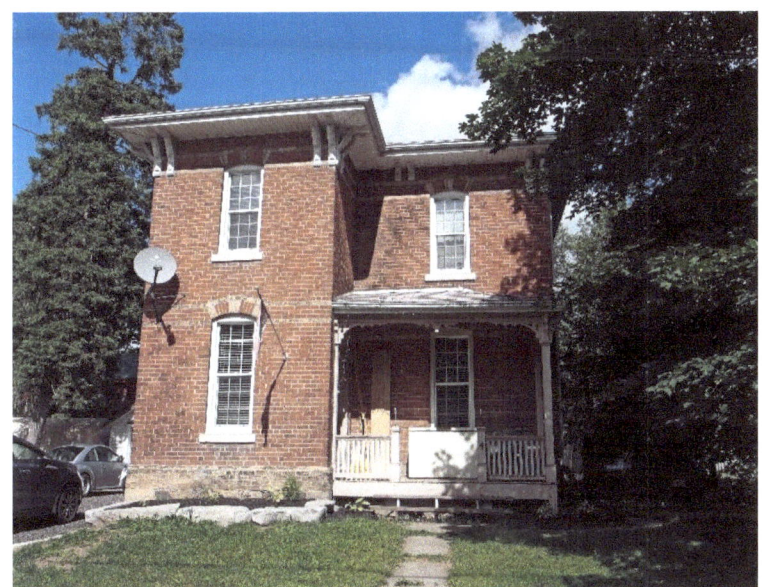

4 Clyde Street – cornice brackets, decorative cornice

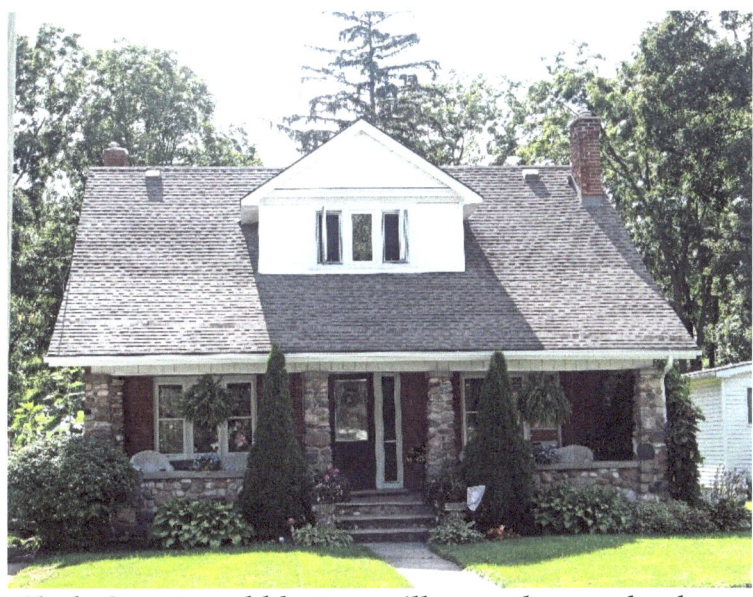

7 Clyde Street – cobblestone pillars and veranda, dormer

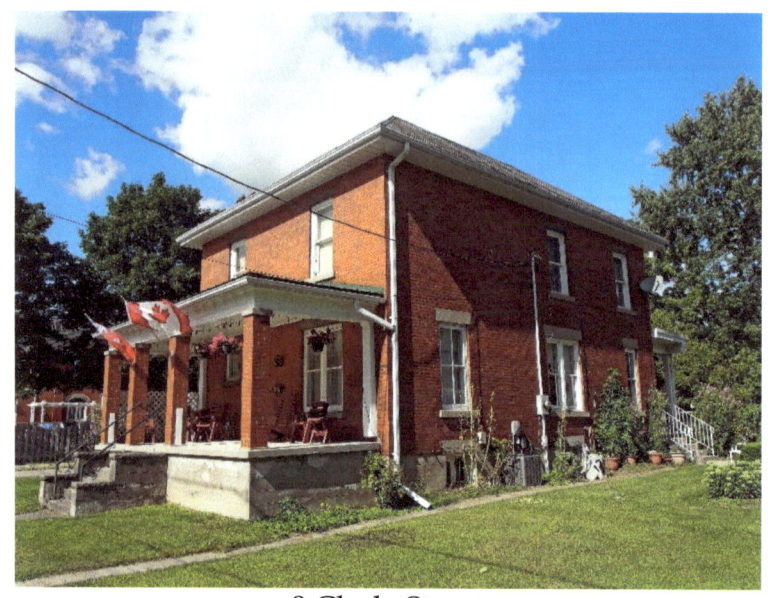

8 Clyde Street

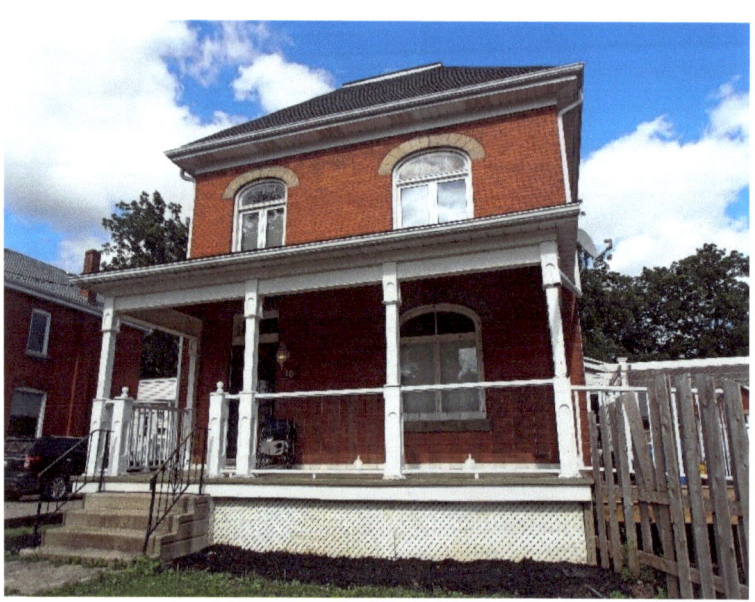

10 Clyde Street - voussoirs

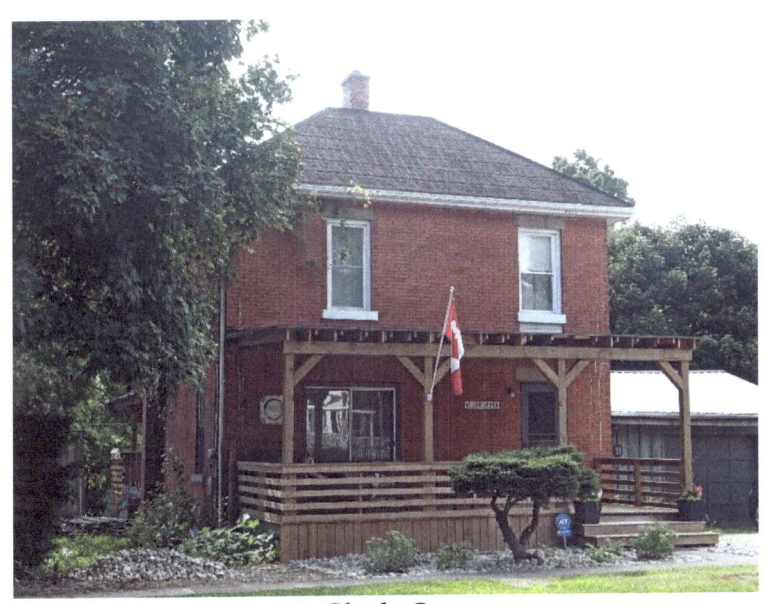

11 Clyde Street

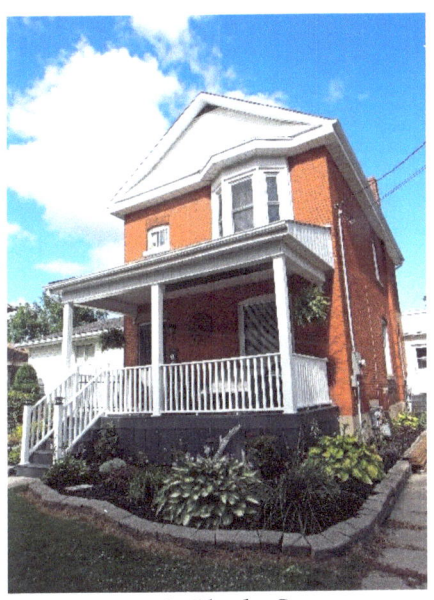

12 Clyde Street

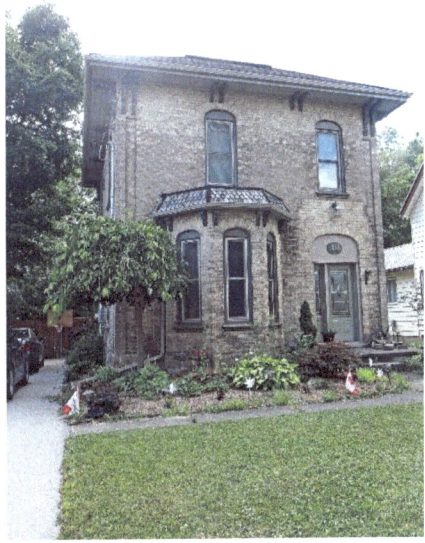

19 Clyde Street
Bay window, cornice brackets

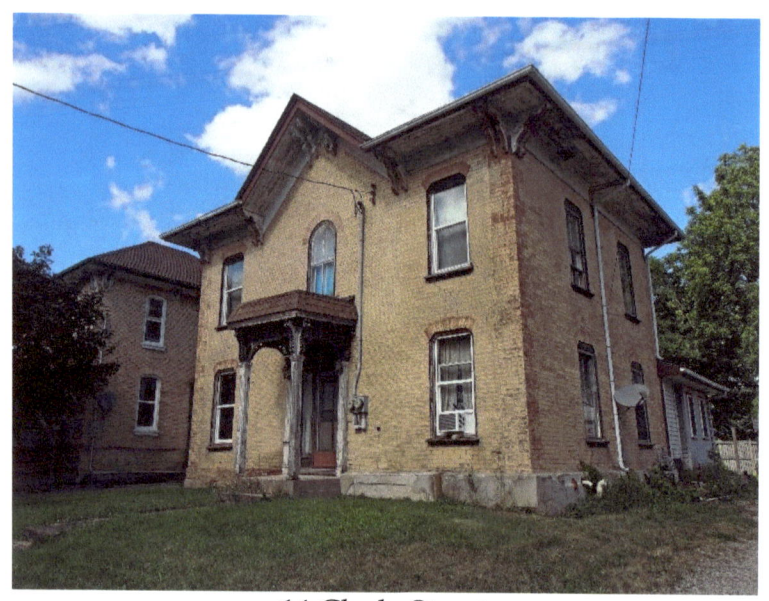
14 Clyde Street

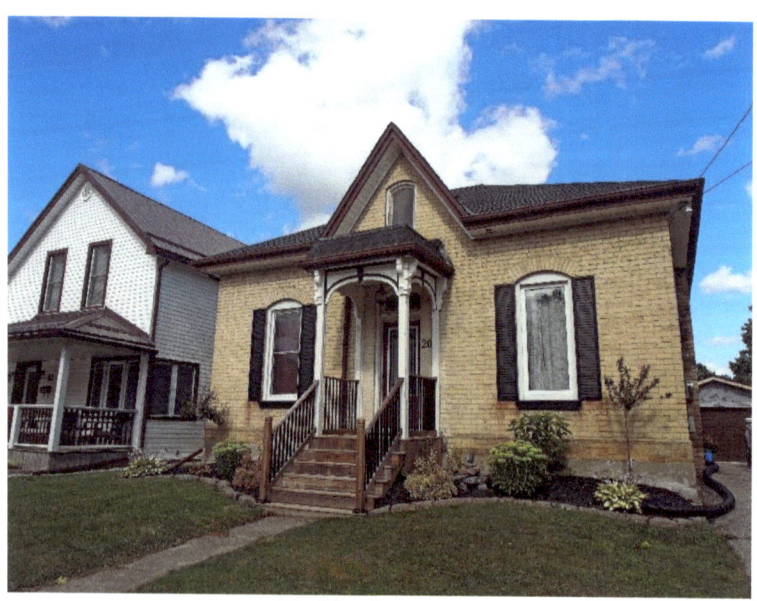
20 Clyde Street

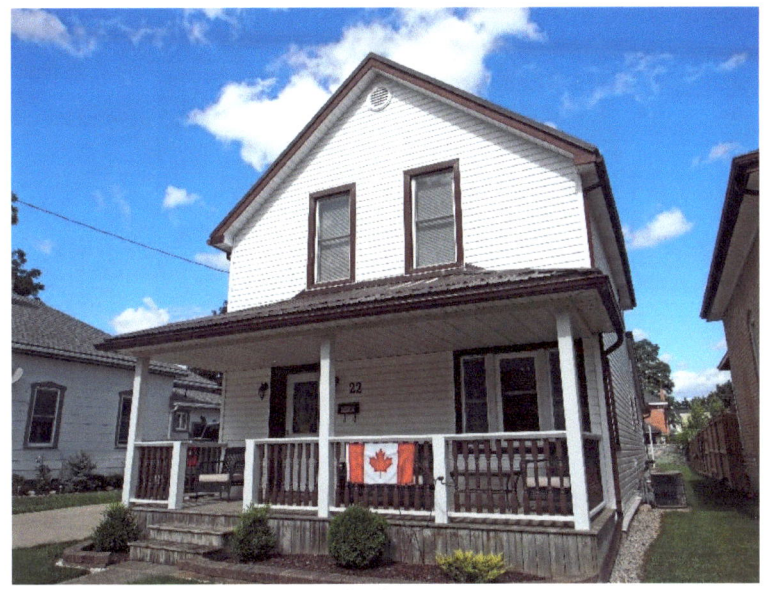

22 Clyde Street

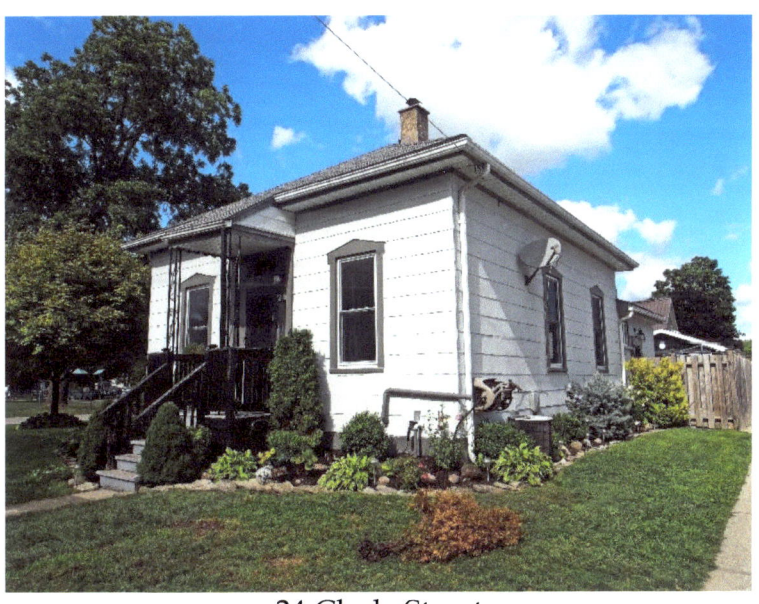

24 Clyde Street

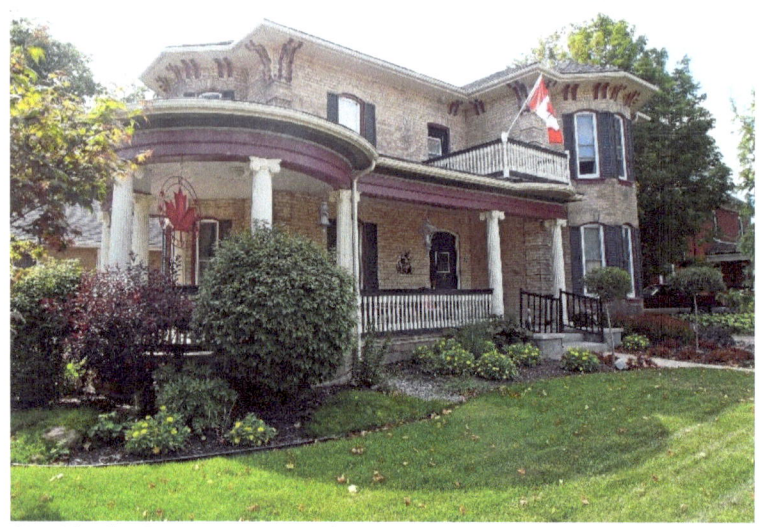

27 Clyde Street – paired cornice brackets, wraparound veranda with Ionic pillars, second-floor balcony

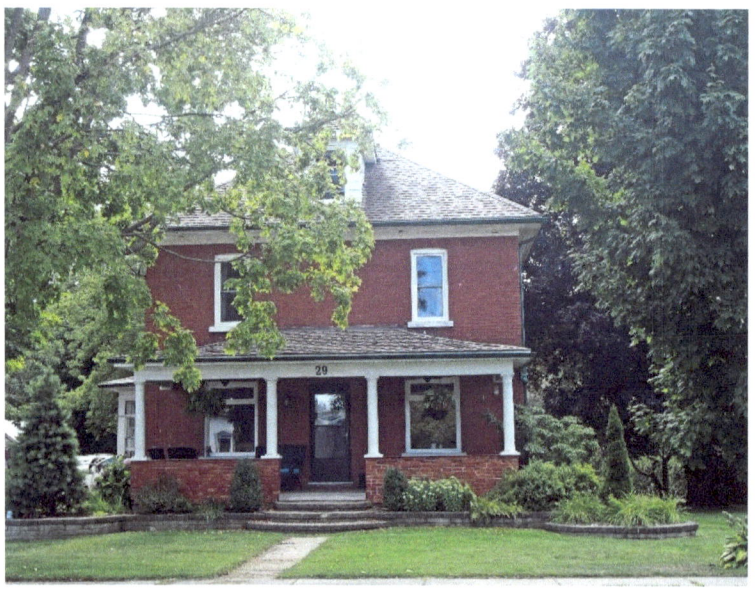

29 Clyde Street

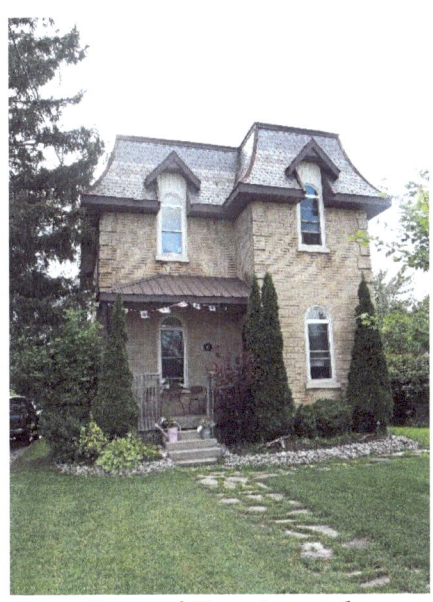

33 Clyde Street – Second Empire style – mansard roof, dormers with window hoods

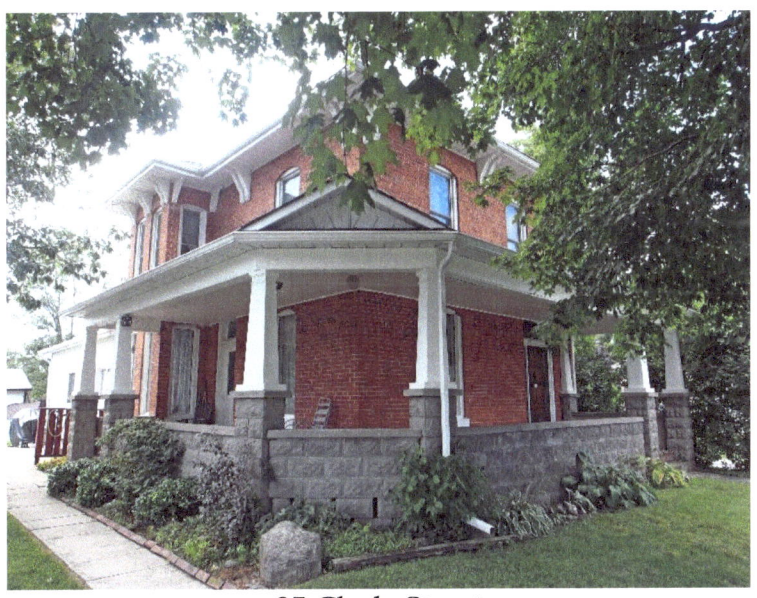

35 Clyde Street

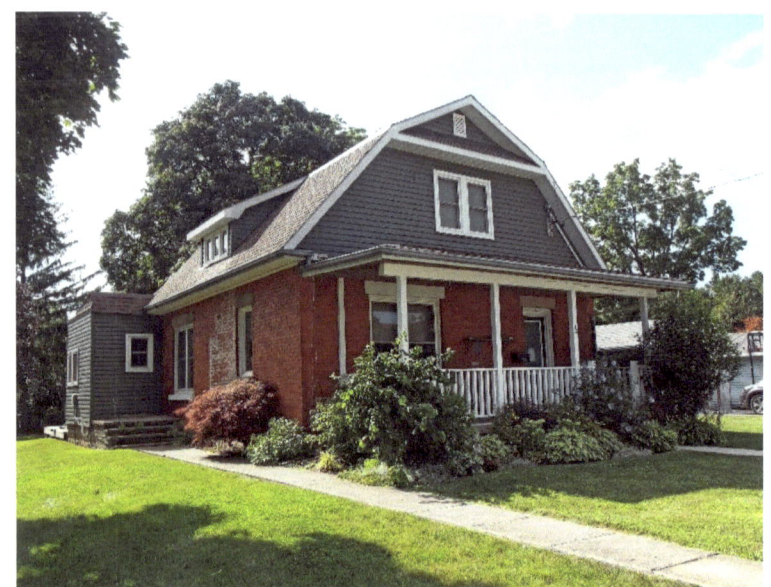

43 Clyde Street – Neo-Colonial – gambrel roof, shed dormer

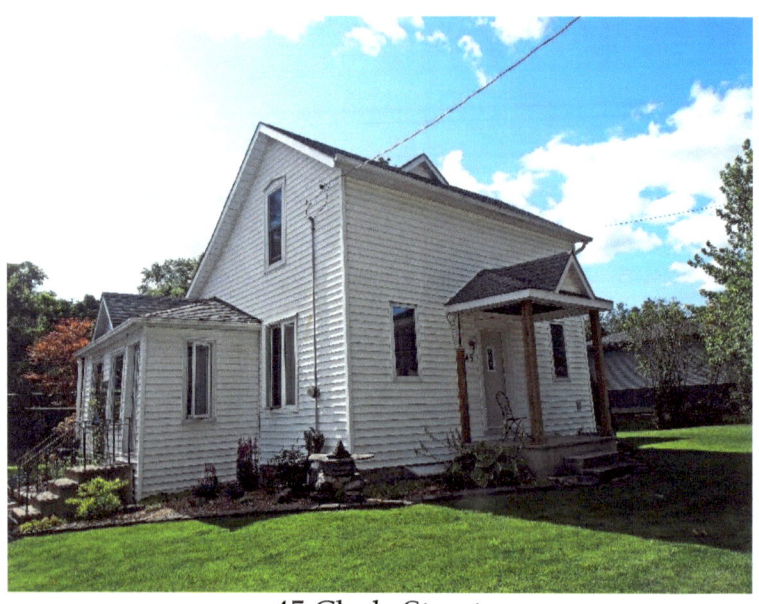

45 Clyde Street

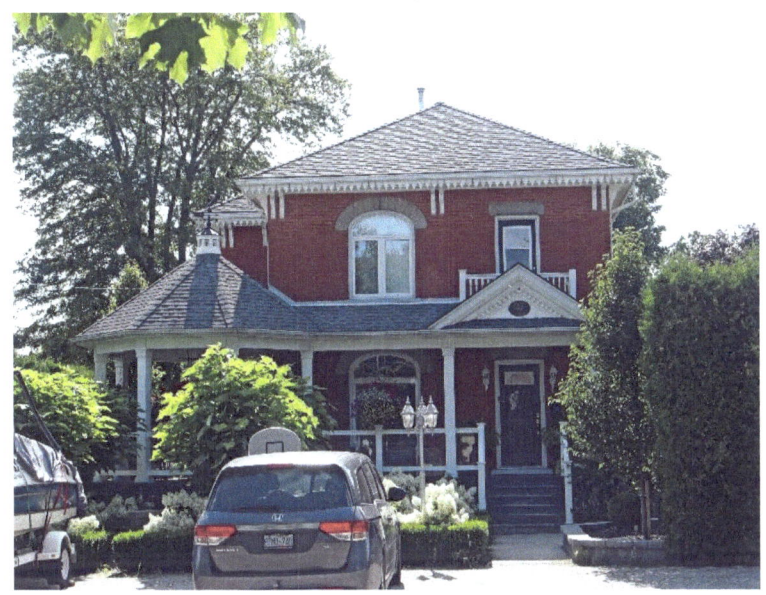

37 John Street – paired cornice brackets

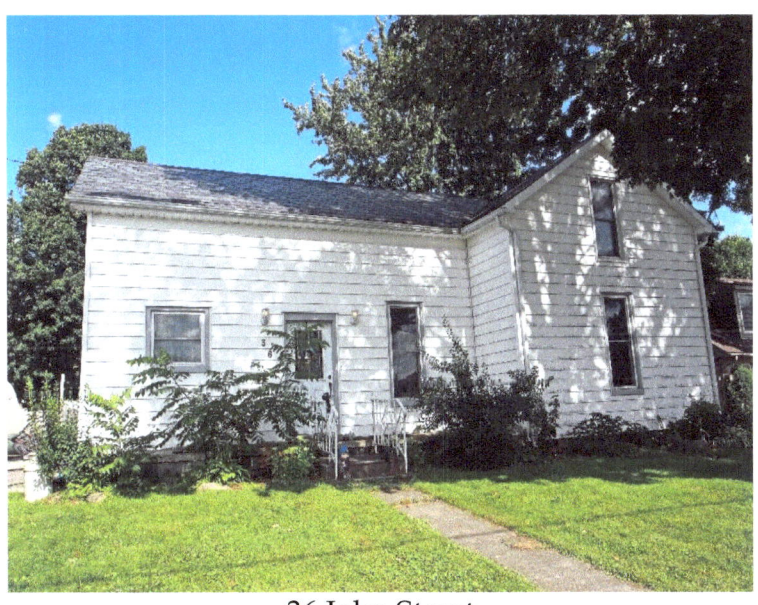

36 John Street

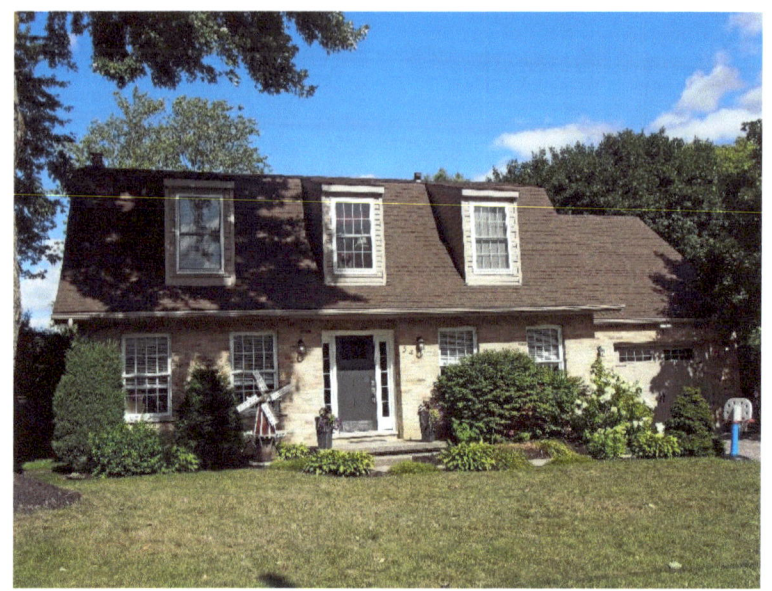
34 John Street - dormers

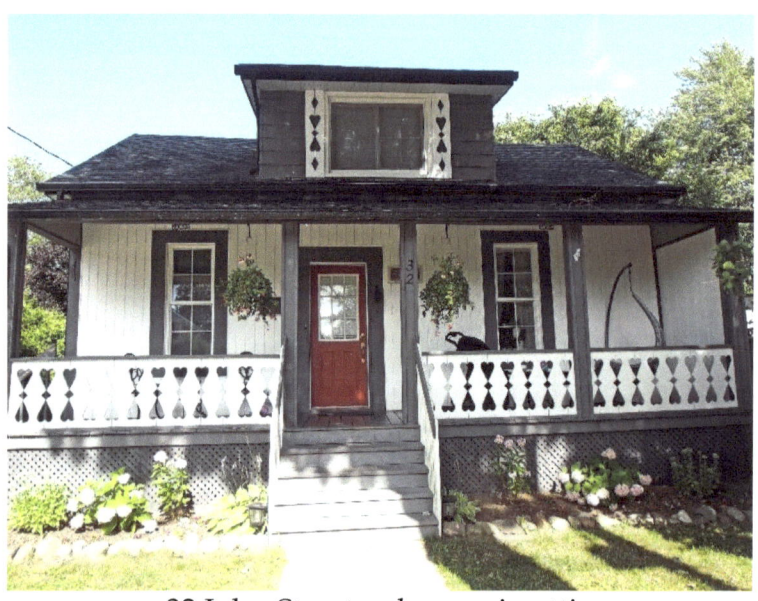
32 John Street – dormer in attic

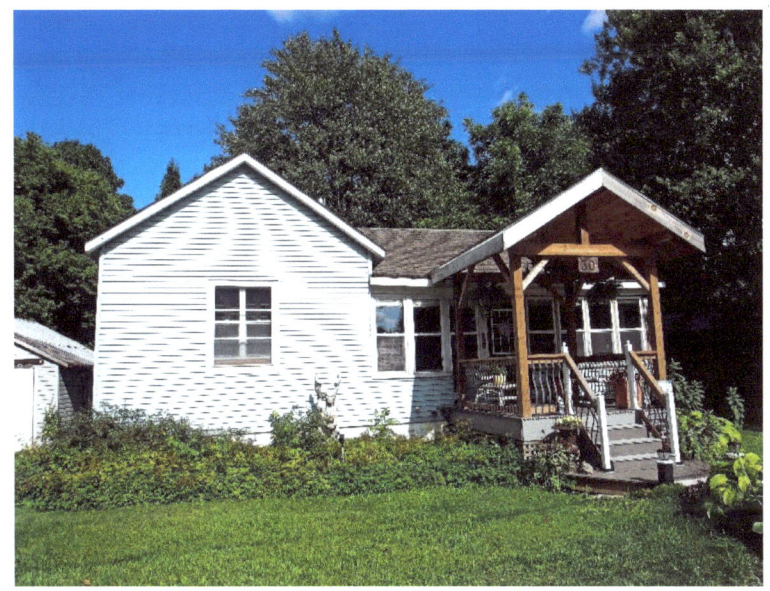

30 John Street

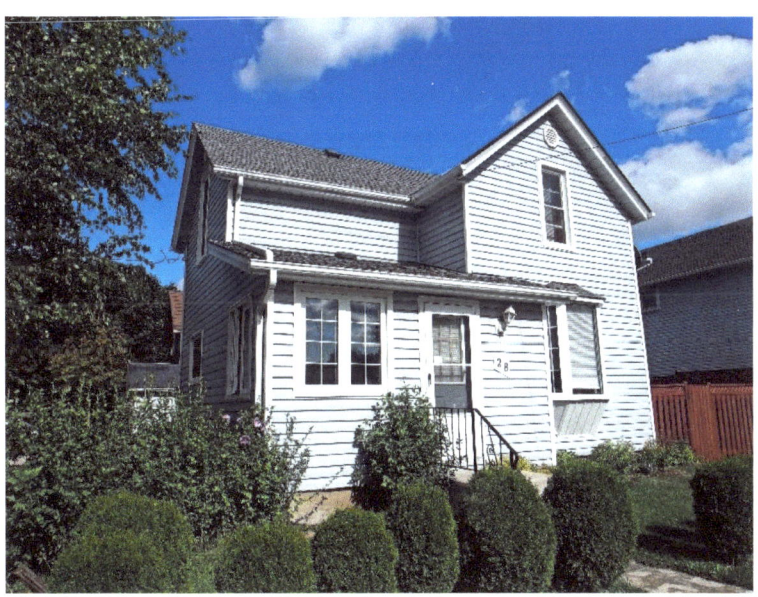

28 John Street

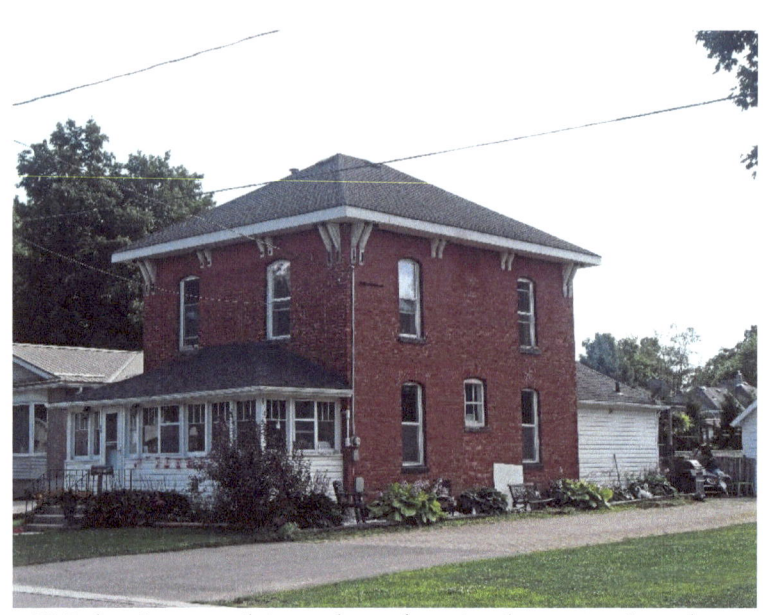
25 John Street – hipped roof, paired cornice brackets

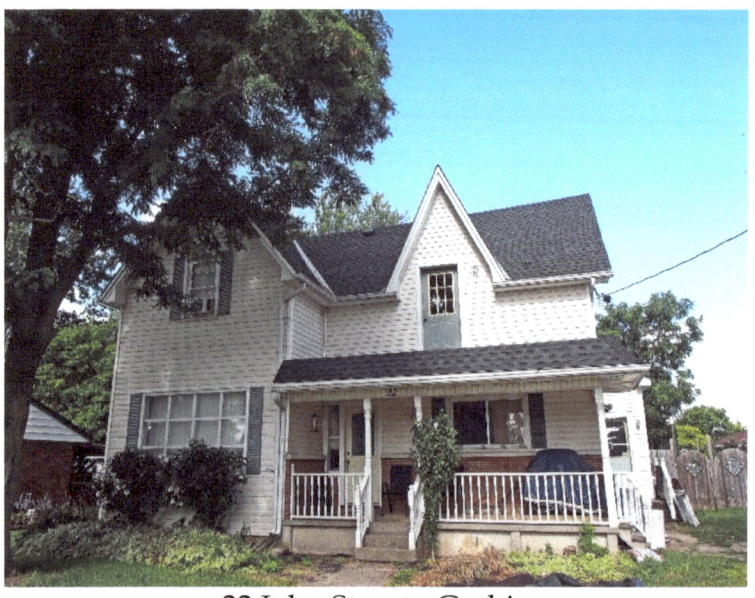
22 John Street - Gothic

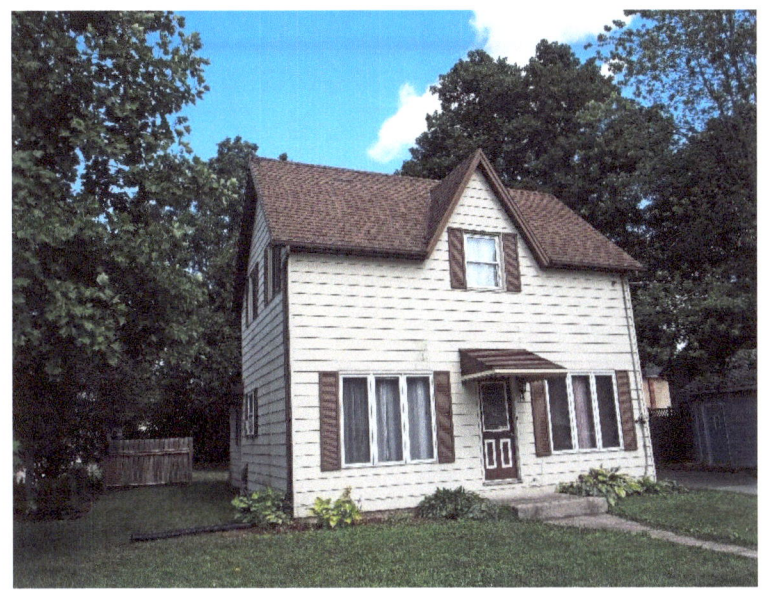

14 John Street - Gothic

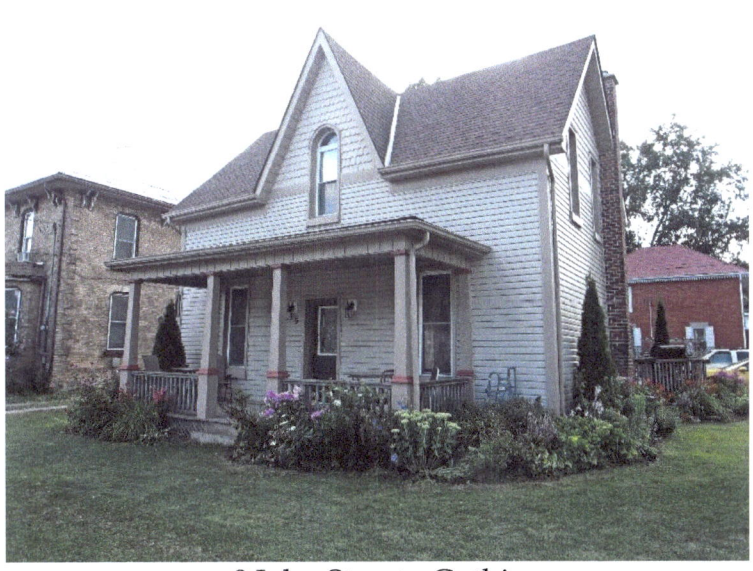

9 John Street - Gothic

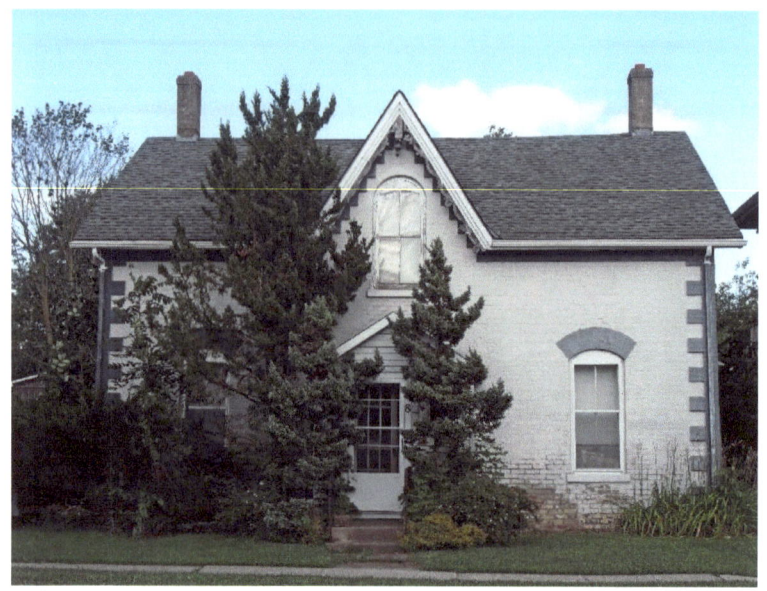

8 John Street – Gothic – verge board trim on gable, corner quoins, voussoirs

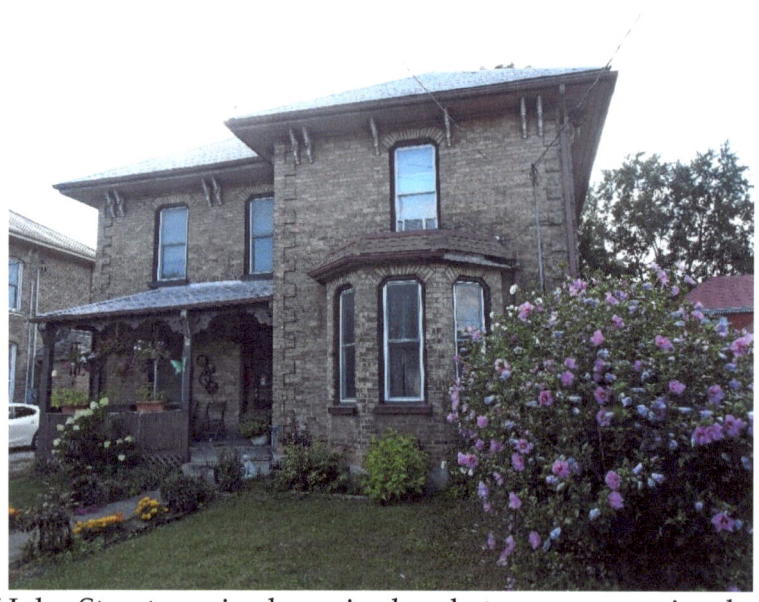

7 John Street – paired cornice brackets, corner quoins, bay window

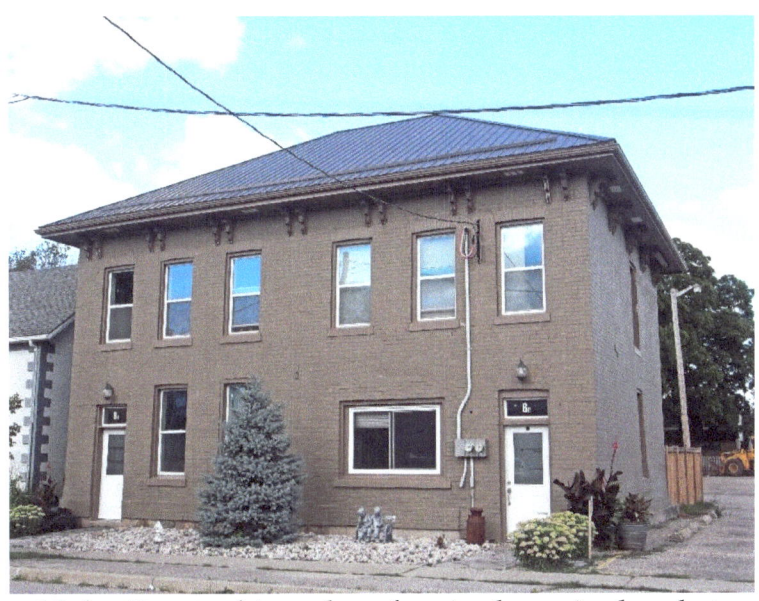

6 John Street – hipped roof, paired cornice brackets

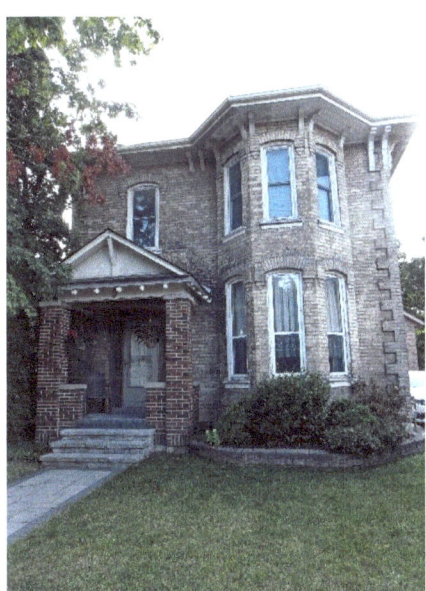

5 John Street
Two-story bay window,
Corner quoins, pediment

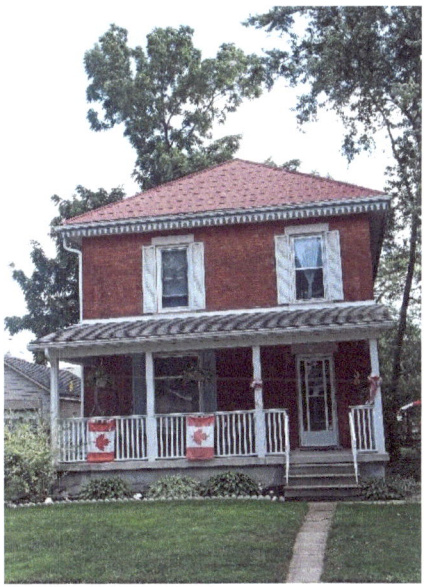

23 Elgin Street West
- full-width veranda

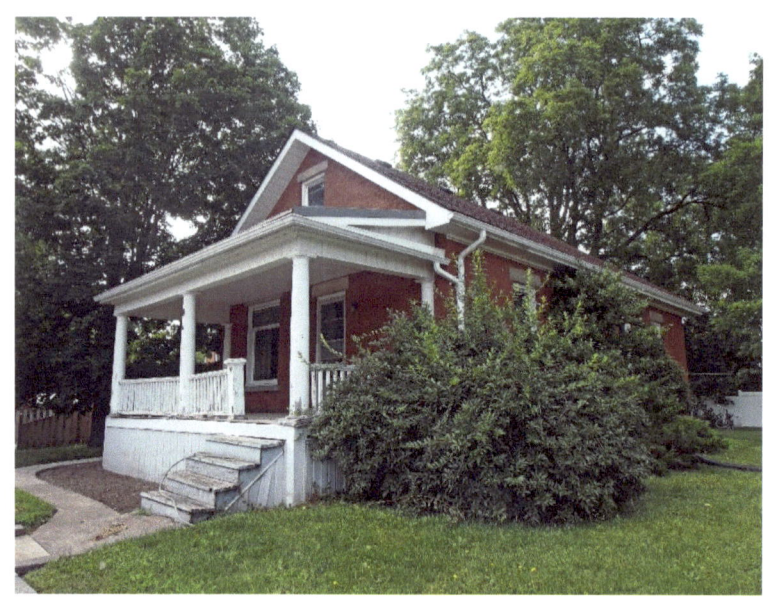

24 Elgin Street West

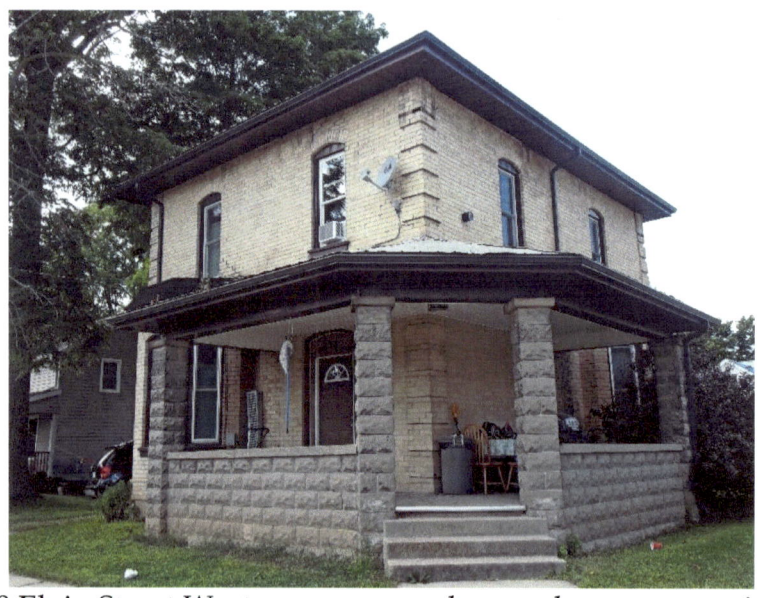

20 Elgin Street West – wraparound veranda, corner quoins

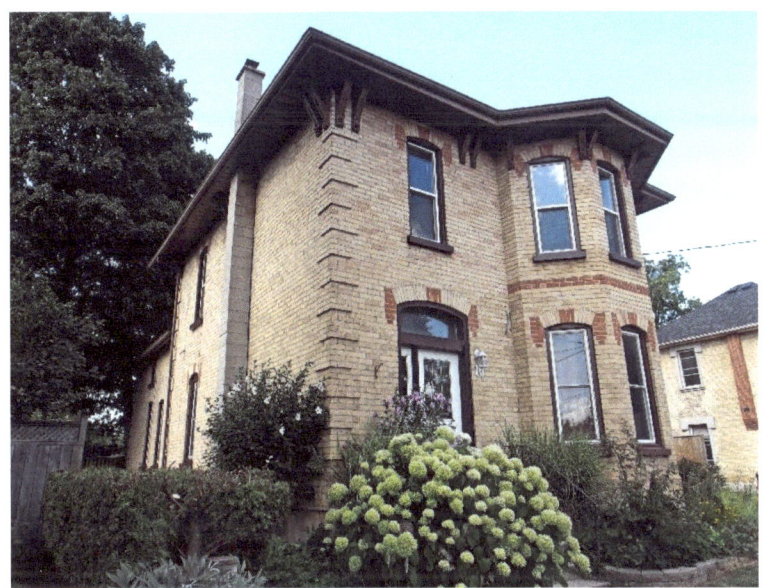

16 Elgin Street West – dichromatic brickwork, two-story bay window, corner quoins, cornice brackets

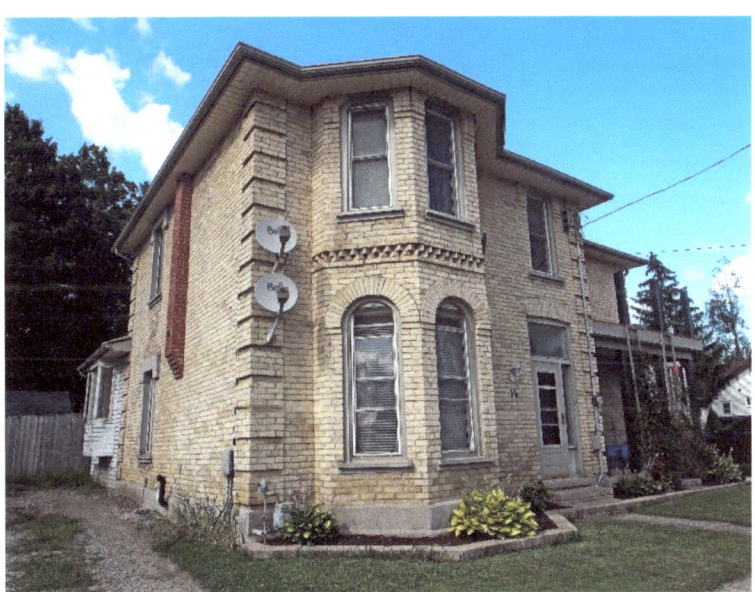

14 Elgin Street West - corner quoins, decorative brickwork

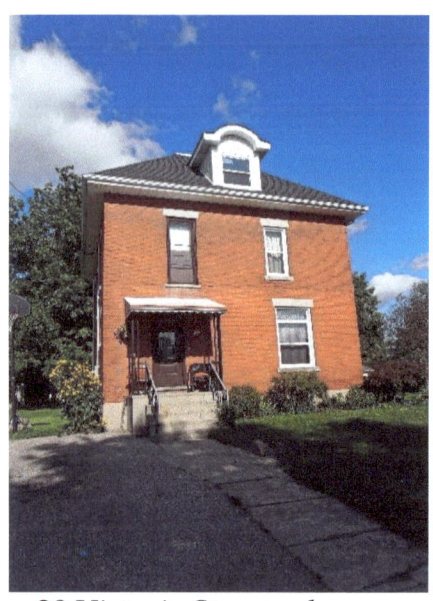
20 Victoria Street - dormer

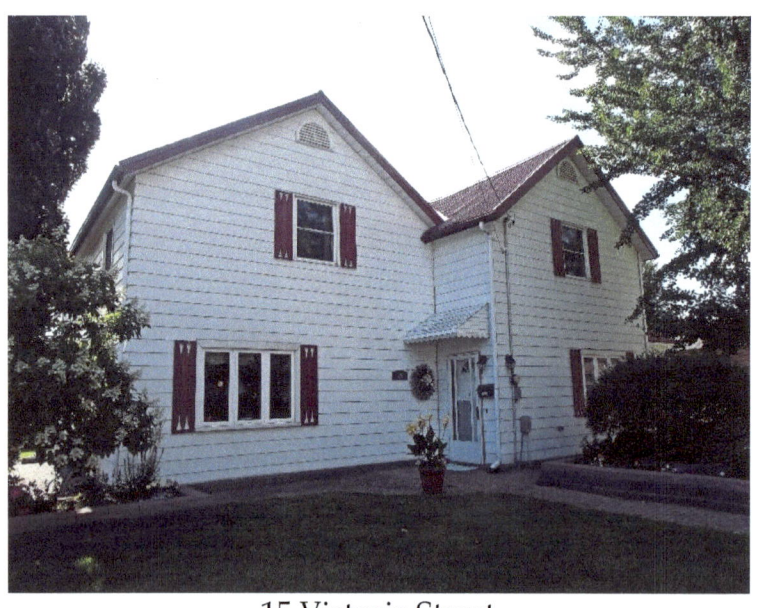
15 Victoria Street

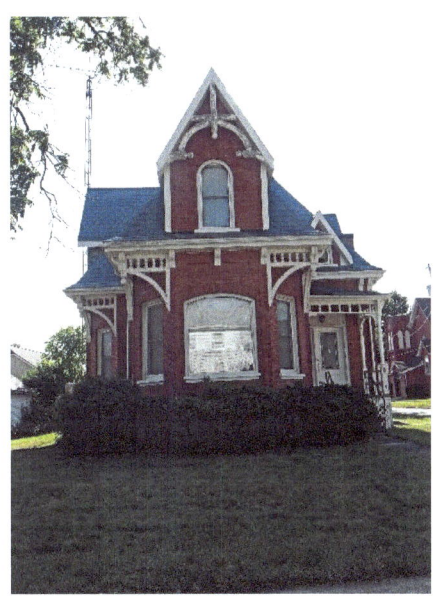

9 Victoria Street

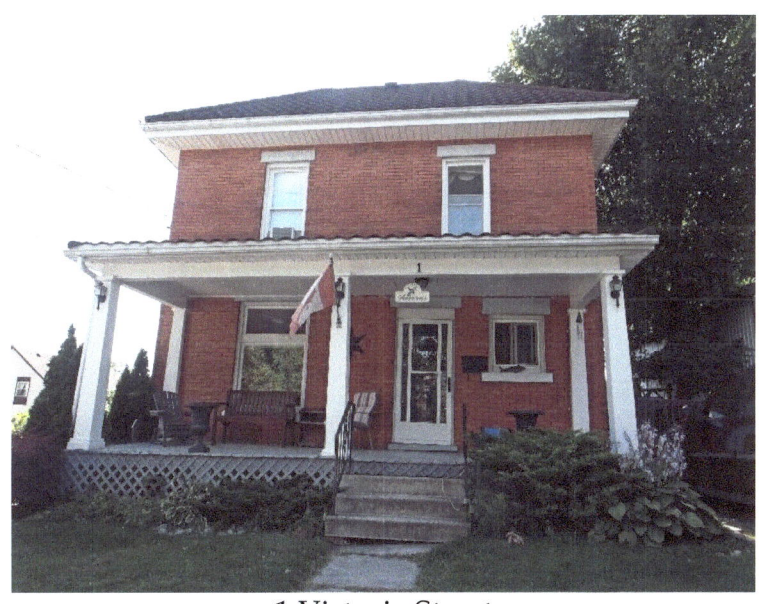

1 Victoria Street

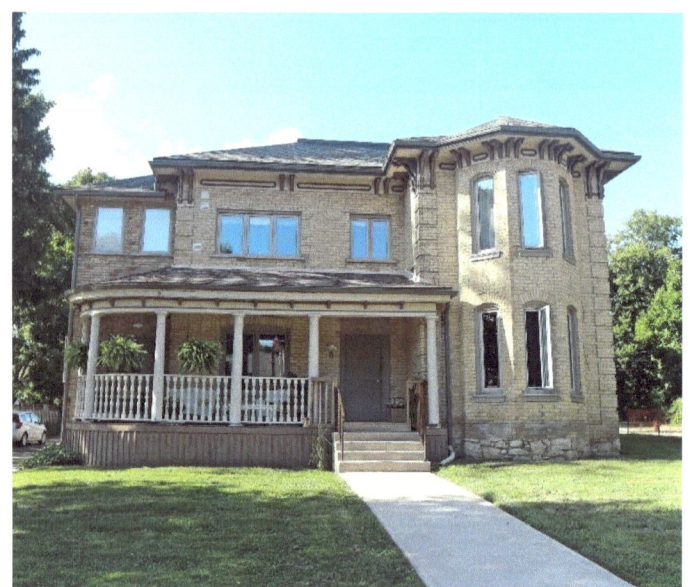

11 Elgin Street East

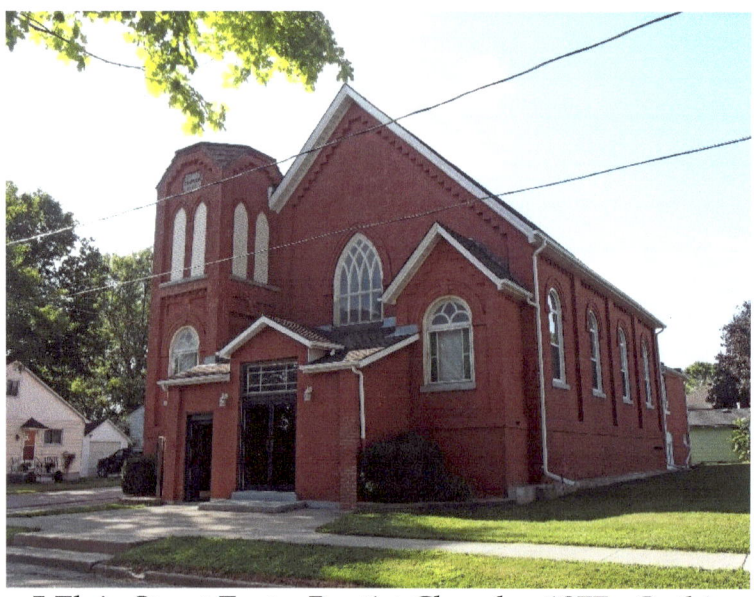

5 Elgin Street East – Baptist Church – 1877 - Gothic

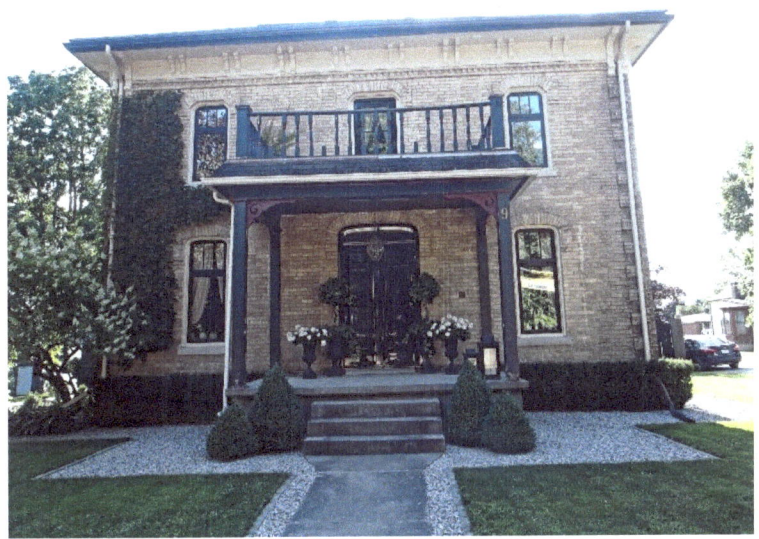

9 Cook Street – Hall/Munro House - built in 1885 - Italianate white brick - centre doorway with frosted sidelights and frosted panels in the door. Window and door surrounds echo the rounded shapes of openings and complement the elaborate brickwork and oval molded panels under the eaves

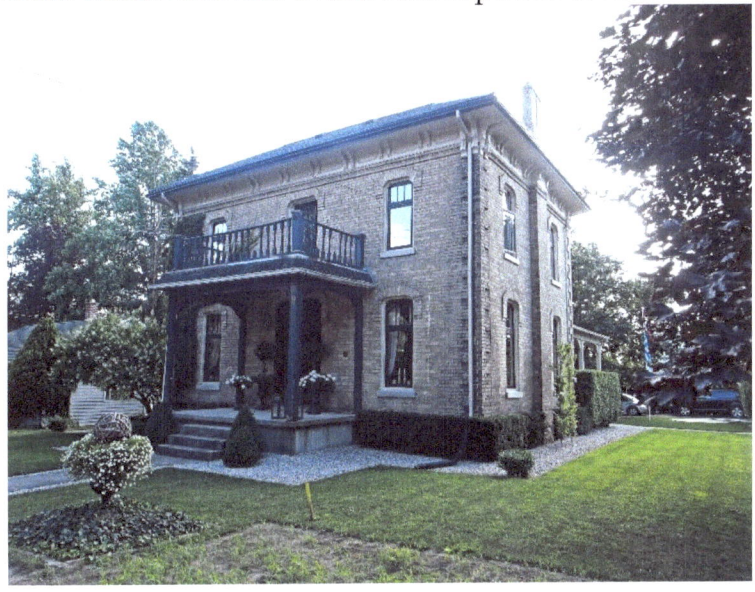

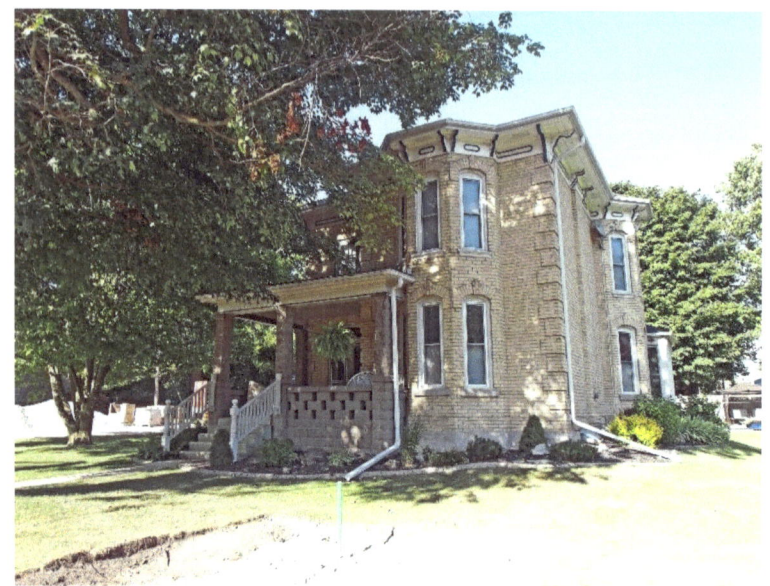

10 Cook Street – Italianate, decorative cornice and brackets, two-story bay window, corner quoins

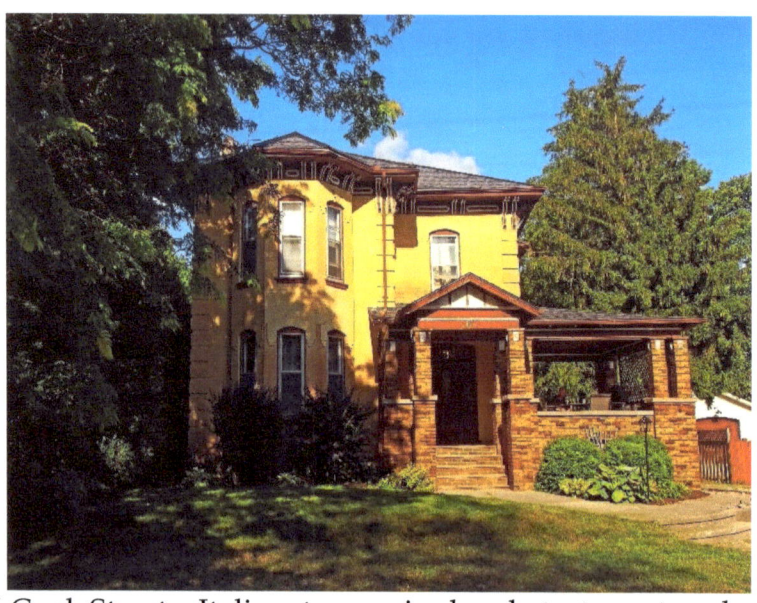

6 Cook Street – Italianate, cornice brackets, two-story bay window, corner quoins, pediment

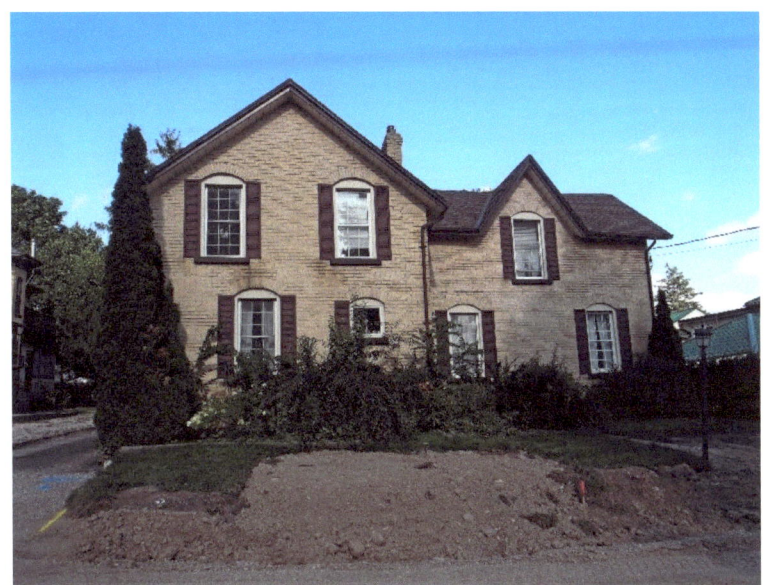

Cook Street - Gothic

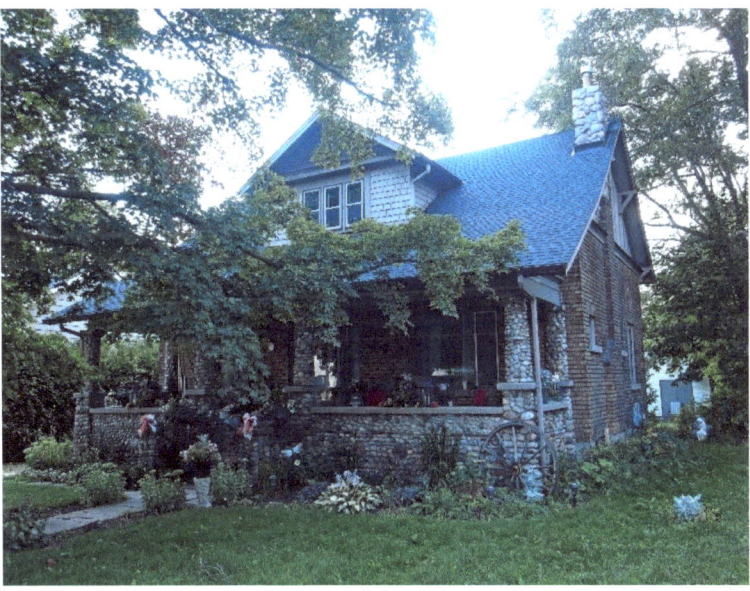

Cook Street – dormer, cobblestone pillars and veranda

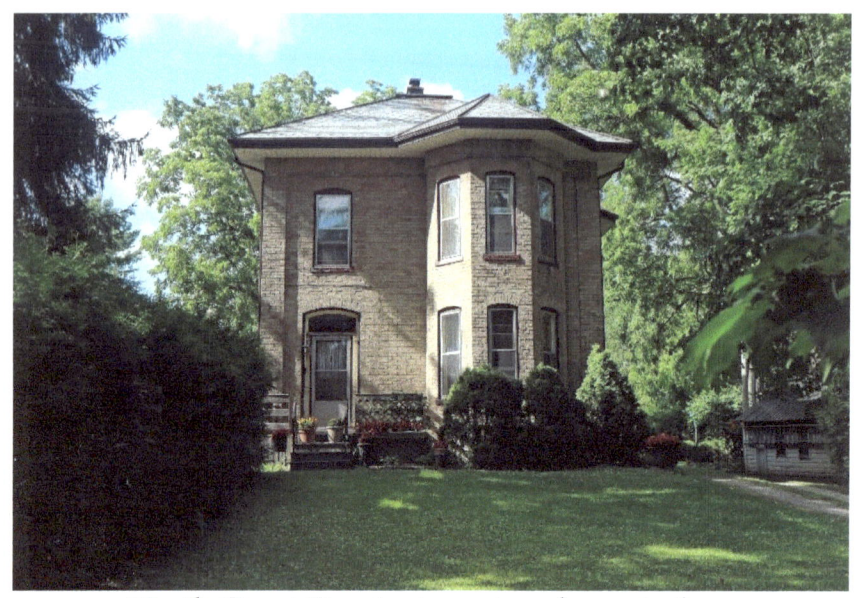

North Court Street – two-story bay window

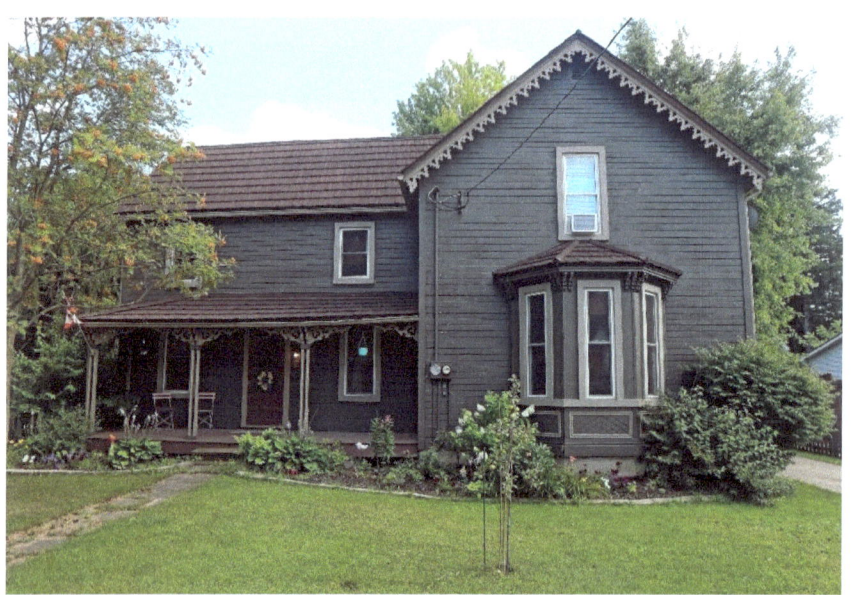

9 North Court Street – Gothic – verge board trim on gable, bay window

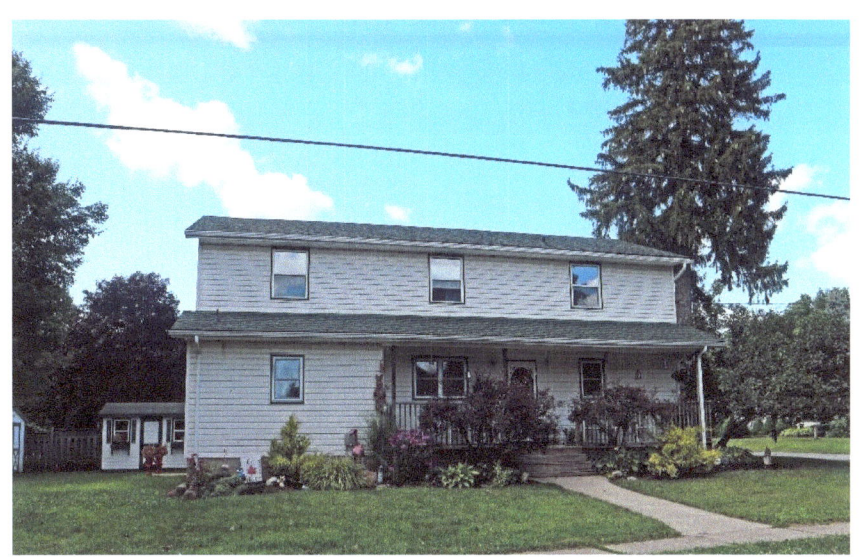

North Court Street

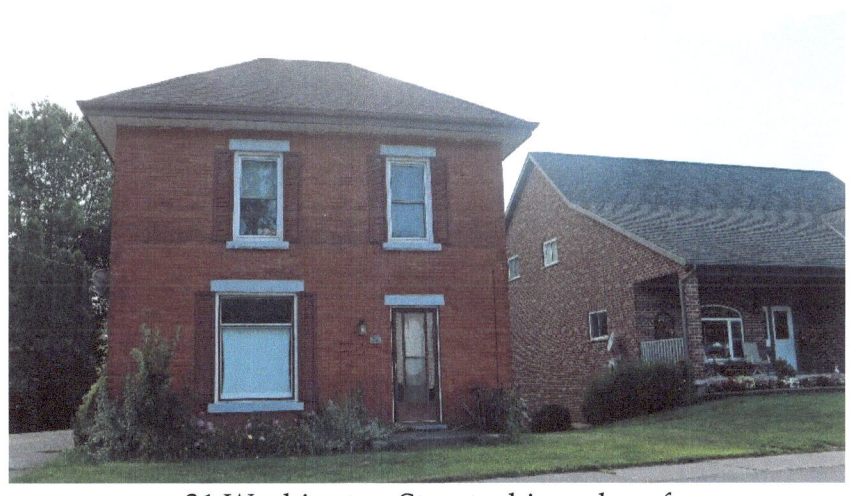

31 Washington Street – hipped roof

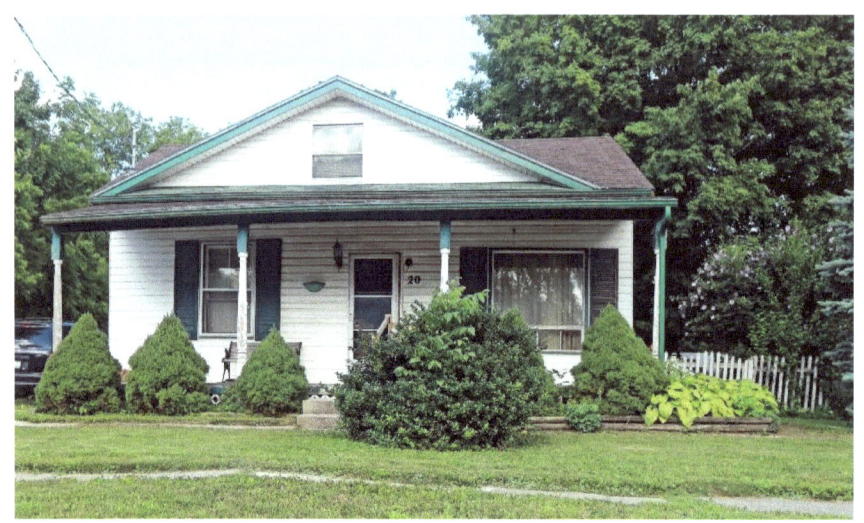

20 Washington Street

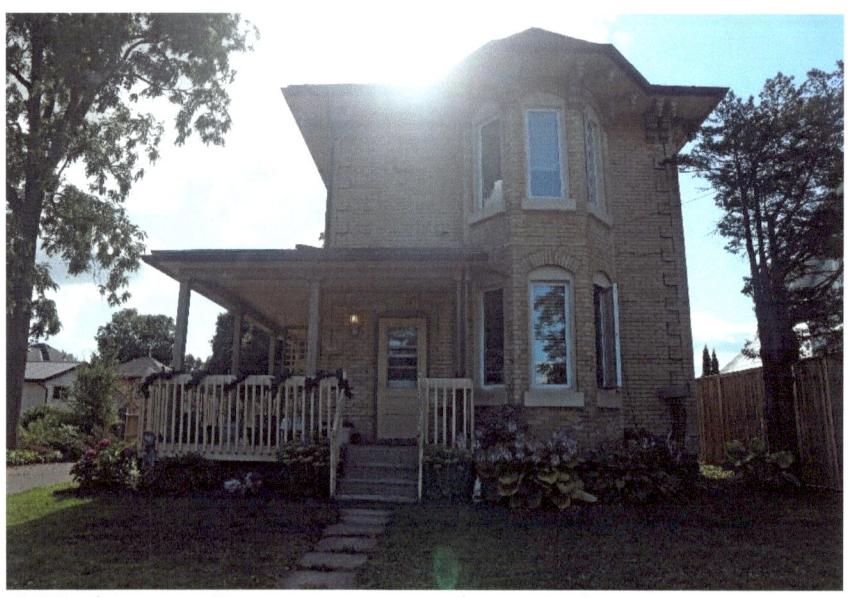

9 Washington Street – two-story bay window, corner quoins

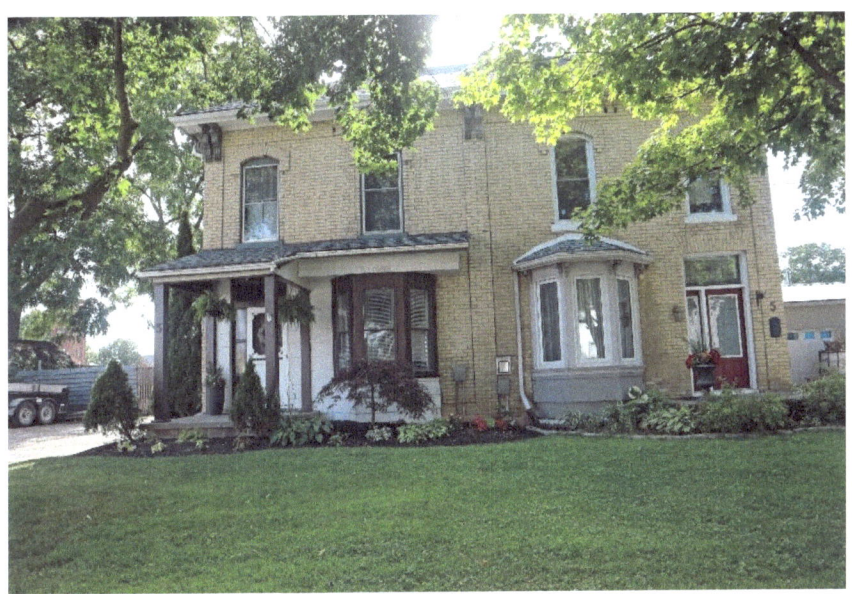

5 Washington Street – cornice brackets, bay window

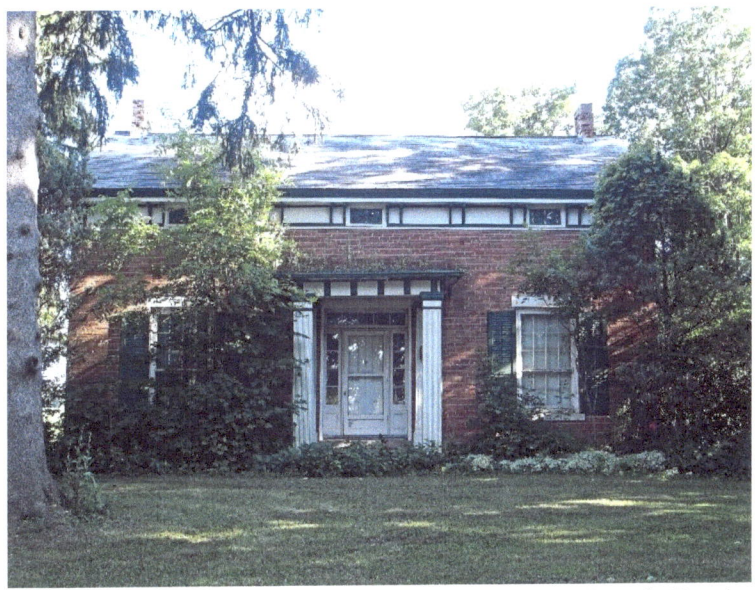

345458 Quaker Street – Sutton/Clark House - Greek Revival - original section ca. 1850, is in the back. The front portion house was added ten years later.

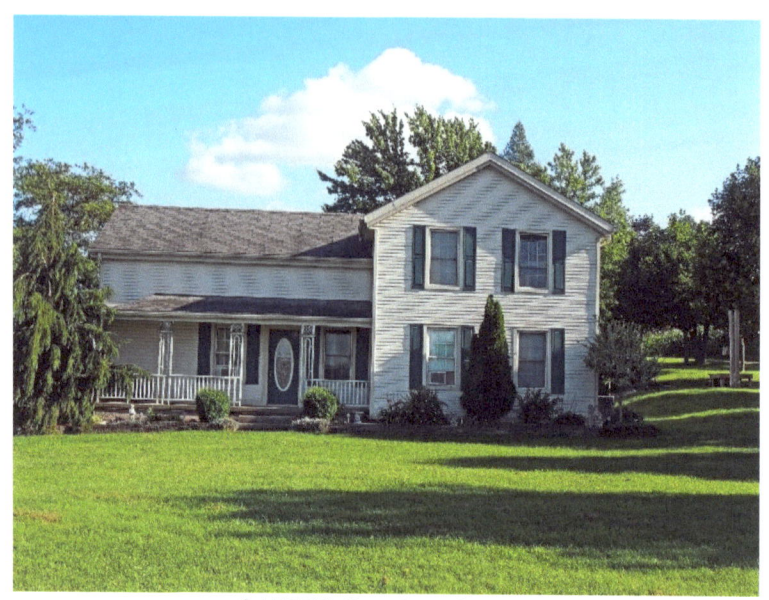

345500 Quaker Street

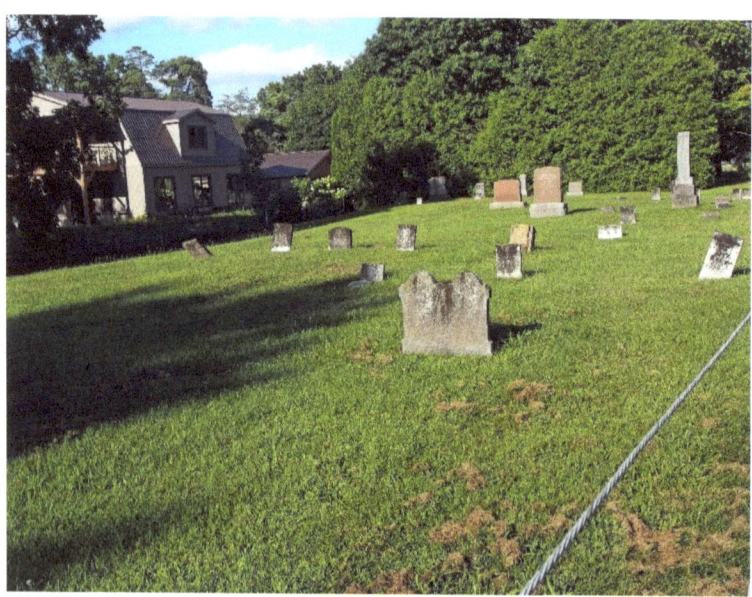

345705 Quaker Street - North Norwich Pioneer Cemetery (Tompkin's Burying Ground) – earliest burial was in 1816

Other Books by Barbara Raue

Coins of Gold
Arrows, Indians and Love
The Life and Times of Barbara
The Cromwell Family Book
Laura Secord Discovered
Daddy Where Are You?

Montana Series
Book 1: Montana Dream
Book 2: Life on the Montana Frontier
Book 3: Montana to Boston and Back
Book 4: Montana Sons Go to War
Book 5: Montana Sons Return from War

Book 1: Rite of Passage
Book 2: Rite of Marriage

© 2019 by Barbara Raue - All the photos in this book have been taken with my cameras. I own the rights to them.

www.ingramcontent.com/pod-product-compliance
Lightning Source LLC
Chambersburg PA
CBHW040229220526
45473CB00001B/176